Mumbai Under Siege

26/11—What Happened and What Went Wrong?

Nikhil S. Dixit

JAICO PUBLISHING HOUSE

Ahmedabad Bangalore Chennai
Delhi Hyderabad Kolkata Mumbai

Published by Jaico Publishing House
A-2 Jash Chambers, 7-A Sir Phirozshah Mehta Road
Fort, Mumbai - 400 001
jaicopub@jaicobooks.com
www.jaicobooks.com

MUMBAI UNDER SIEGE
ISBN 978-81-7992-995-7

First Jaico Impression: 2009
Second Jaico Impression: 2009

Printed by
Trinity Academy For Corporate Training Limited, Mumbai

Dedication

This book is dedicated to the brave men of the Mumbai police force and the NSG, who laid down their lives while fighting the *fidayeens*, and the innocent victims of the November 26, 2008 terror attacks in Mumbai.

Acknowledgments

This book could not have been completed without the help of many of my friends, some of whom are policemen.

I would also wish to thank:

My executive editor, R Jagannathan, who was kind enough to grant me permission to go ahead with the book.

My boss, B Mahesh, who was extremely supportive of my endeavour and encouraged me to complete this task.

My present employer, DNA, for being patient with me and allowing me to devote my time and energy on writing this book.

I am greatly indebted to senior journalist and my professor, Mr Abhay Mokashi, who has been, and always will be, my inspiration.

Expressing any amount of gratitude will be too little when

it comes to thanking my wife Sweta, a far better journalist and writer than me, who not only inspired me to write this book, but also helped me complete it. She had to bear all the long hours that I spent in front of the computer and all the mess in the house with reports strewn everywhere. I thank her for being patient and understanding.

I also wish to thank my parents for supporting and encouraging me to go ahead with this book.

A special thanks to J Dey and Dev Chatterjee. Without their support this book would have not been possible.

Many thanks to Ayaz Memon, Sanjay Vhanmane, Prabhakar Pawar, Calvin Joshua, Neelesh Dixit, Gautam Ramanujan, Dhiraj Gopalani, S P Nauriyal, and Leslie Pereira who gave me the help I needed to complete this book.

Prologue

Lest We Forget

Mumbai will perhaps never forget the night of November 26, 2008. It took only a few minutes for this city, known for its never-say-die attitude and a vibrant nightlife, to turn into the city of Death.

Making their way to Mumbai from Karachi in Pakistan, ten *fidayeens* used the cover of darkness to sneak into the city and mercilessly kill 165 innocents, including a top cop from the anti-terror cell of the Mumbai police. This terrible incident not only exposed various chinks in the Indian security system, but also showed how uncaring authorities are about the lives of common people.

This was not the first time that the city was ravaged so brutally. Just two years ago, in 2006, a series of bomb blasts ripped apart the lifeline of Mumbai – the local trains – killing more than 174 people who were making their way home after work.

No lessons were learnt either from 2006 or from any other terror attack on the city and in other parts of the country. One feels that there would perhaps be no takeaways from the 26/11 attack as well. Mumbai is the most cosmopolitan city in India with its people welcoming migrants irrespective of their caste, creed, religion etc. Though there are a few politicians who try to sow the seeds of enmity based on language, and religion, most Mumbaikars prefer to mind their own business.

Mumbai generates so much income in a year that it contributes to almost 40 per cent of the country's tax kitty. No wonder then, the city is known as the financial capital of the country. The city is home to billionaires, slum dwellers, and millions belonging to the working class. Over six million people travel to work every day by trains, buses, and private transport. The standard of living for the majority is not very good, and yet they come to work with a smile every day.

The Pakistan-based Lashkar-e-Toiba (LeT) *fidayeens* brought the city to its knees by attacking Leopold Café, a popular restaurant and bar frequented by western tourists; the most luxurious and expensive hotels – The Taj and Oberoi-Trident – regular haunts for the city's glitterati and corporate bigwigs; and the Chhatrapati Shivaji Terminus (CST), a heritage structure and one of the most crowded and busiest railway stations in the world. They also killed a rabbi and his wife at Nariman House, home to a few members of the orthodox Jewish group, Chabad Lubavitch.

The *fidayeens'* motive was to gain maximum publicity and maim the city's spirit. However, within days, the Taj and Oberoi had re-opened for business. Ratan Tata, Chairman of the Taj Group of hotels said, "We can be hurt but we cannot be knocked down." Mr Tata's words summed up the sentiments of millions of Mumbaikars.

What is most worrying is that after 9/11, Islamic fundamentalist groups led by Al Qaeda – unemployed after the Afghanistan war – joined hands with Kashmiri militants and found a common enemy in India. Since then, a series of bomb blasts across all major Indian cities has killed and maimed thousands. Such attacks have been increasing since 2008. In an attack in Ahmedabad, in the state of Gujarat, in July, 55 people were killed, in September, serial bomb blasts in Delhi (India's capital) laid claim to 20 lives. Mumbai was probably just another destination in their terrible itinerary.

The U.S. government never treated the *fidayeen* attacks in India the way they would have treated bombings in Madrid, Bali, or London. The Federal Bureau of Investigation (FBI) the U.S's premier investigation agency always maintained that the problem in India was a local one or 'homegrown'. They meant that local Muslim groups with help from Pakistan-based terror outfits were fighting the local population. They did not see it as part of America's war on terror.

The attacks in Mumbai have proved that theory wrong. Mumbai is now on the global terror map and it will be some time before a foreign national can feel safe while sipping beer at popular tourist haunts such as Leopold Café.

According to preliminary investigations by the Mumbai police, the ten *fidayeens* began their journey on November 23 from Karachi, in Pakistan, in a small fishing boat. The group then boarded a Pakistani vessel *Al Husseni*, and then hijacked an Indian trawler *MV Kuber* to cross the porous Indian border. The trawler mingled with thousands of other vessels sailing towards Mumbai. Surprisingly, an Indian Navy exercise was on at that time, in those very same waters, to detect infiltration.

By the evening of November 26, the *fidayeens* had landed in Mumbai – slipping past hundreds of Indian Navy and Coast Guard ships. They then made their way to their predetermined destinations by taxi. After 60 hours of chaos and terror, nine *fidayeens* were killed by Indian security forces, and one, Mohammad Ajmal Amir alias Kasab, from Faridkot in Pakistan, was arrested.

The Taj Mahal hotel, which was built by legendary industrialist Jamshetji Tata to avenge an insult by the British who would not let him enter a White-only hotel, was ravaged by a fire that could not be put out for hours. The *fidayeens* perhaps got what they wanted –international headlines – since media persons from across the world came to Mumbai to cover the horror.

Inside the Oberoi-Trident Hotel, the *fidayeens* showed absolutely no mercy towards the victims. Eyewitnesses said that the gunmen had asked them to stand in a queue waiting to be shot, while they spoke to someone on their mobile phones. Their handlers back in Pakistan wanted to hear the gunshots. The killers were laughing and joking, and when the victims asked them why they were doing this, the *fidayeens* reminded them of the atrocities committed during the Babri Masjid demolitions, Jammu and Kashmir and during the Gujarat riots. It was clear that the *fidayeens*, who looked like college kids in their early 20s, were obsessed with retribution for Hindu atrocities against Muslims.

The Special Forces killed the last *fidayeen* in the Taj after a 60-hour gun battle. By then scores of innocents had been killed and Mumbai's pride was severely dented. This book highlights the stories of a few unsung heroes, the officers who laid their life down without a moment's hesitation about their families back home.

Contents

1
A *Fidayeen* Caught Alive

The perennially busy and noisy junction at Girgaum Chowpatty was eerily silent. The night was unusually quiet. The brightly lit road, which on any other day would be full of people crowding around food stalls, was empty as if it was haunted. Only the shadows of the heavily armed and nervous policemen could be seen.

Residents of the buildings opposite Girgaum Chowpatty were not used to the deathly silence on the road below. With 'breaking news' of heavily armed terrorists creating havoc in the city, people were glued to their television sets, trying to get the latest on the mayhem.

When it was clear that South Mumbai was the main target, jittery residents chose to remain indoors and catch the action live on television. An occasional car would tear through the road, it would be stopped by the police. Weary residents would peep through their windows while the police checked the car and told the driver that no one was allowed into South Mumbai.

A few minutes after midnight, the police suddenly swung into action. Their walkie-talkies crackled to life and brief instructions were given. Police constables ran from one end of the road to the other trying to place enough heavy, rusted iron barricades to seal the road.

The entire junction was turned into a fortress within minutes, making the residents even more anxious. "The gunmen have hijacked a silver-colour Skoda car and it is heading your way," reported the voice on the walkie-talkie in Marathi. The barricades across the road ensured that not even a bicycle could pass through, an unusual sight, but given the situation, this probably was a very wise decision.

The 20-odd policemen from the local D B Marg police station found themselves in a bizarre situation. They were trained to handle millions of people who throng the Girgaum Chowpatty every year for immersing Ganpati idols. They weren't trained to handle terrorists on the run.

The policemen armed with their archaic .303 rifles, revolvers, batons, and lathis placed themselves at strategic positions and waited with bated breath. Among them was 48-year-old Assistant Sub-Inspector – Tukaram Omble – armed with a lathi and a wireless set. He would have passed off as any other *tumbaku* (tobacco) chewing police officer, but Omble was about to create history.

Interestingly, Omble was that night standing at the very place where he had stood a few months ago to help people fight off jelly fishes that had floated ashore from the Arabian Sea.

The silence was once again broken by the crackle of the walkie-talkie, the voice on the other side said that the Skoda had passed Marine Drive and would reach them at any moment. "It has to be stopped under any circumstance," instructed the voice.

The nervous policemen once again checked their positions and waited, as their sweaty palms gripped their guns.

Their hearts started racing as sounds of a car approaching the junction at breakneck speed tore through the eerie silence. The well-lit road was now even brighter with the blazing headlights of the car zooming towards them.

But it screeched to a halt about 50 meters in front of the barricades and the headlights were switched off. It was as if the people inside were contemplating their next move. To ensure that there were no innocent citizens in the car, a police officer spoke through a loudspeaker and told the occupants of the car to get out and start walking towards the police, with their hands in the air.

But, no one moved. Those few moments of silence stretched towards eternity, while each side waited for the other to act first. Since no one got out of the car in spite of the warning, the policemen were now sure that this was the car they were warned about. Suddenly, the headlights blazed on, almost blinding the cops and the car instantly accelerated as if it were in an Formula One motor race.

The car had almost reached maximum speed as it neared the barricades and before the policemen could react, it turned right, towards the divider, in an attempt to cross to the other side. But, the front wheel of the car got caught in the divider, taking the driver by surprise.

Seizing the opportunity, the police team started firing at the car, but the driver (later identified as Ismail Khan) instantly responded with a shower of bullets from his sophisticated AK-47 assault rifle.

Omble was standing at the other end of the road from where he had a clear view of the other occupant in the front seat. Maintaining his composure, Omble quickly took stock of the situation. He had seen that the other gunman was struggling to shoot from his AK-47 rifle. Seizing the opportunity, Omble leapt towards the gunman and reaching through the window, grabbed the rifle with one hand and tried to open the door with the other.

The gunman had bullet injuries on both his hands. Ajmal was finding it difficult to hold on to the gun. As Omble tried to grab it, Ajmal pressed the trigger with his thumb and five bullets pierced Omble's body.

As his blood flowed away, Omble held on to the gun and grabbed it as he fell to the ground. But, still, the police constable had not eased the pressure on the gun. This forced the gunman out of the car and to his knees, giving the other policemen an opportunity to overpower the unarmed gunman, while Omble collapsed to the ground.

Meanwhile, other policemen, including Sub-Inspectors Bhaskar Kadam, Sanjay Govilkar, and Assistant Police

Inspector Hemant Bavdhankar were engaged in a gun battle with Ismail, which finally ended with the terrorists death.

The entire incident was over in a few minutes, but in those few minutes, Omble had pulled off a feat unmatched anywhere in the world. He had caught a dreaded *fidayeen* (suicide bomber) – Mohammad Ajmal Amir alias Kasab – alive.

Born to a farmer in Satara district of Maharashtra, Omble was the youngest of four children. He is survived by his wife and four daughters.

His bravery helped the nation considerably, because Ajmal is alive and India and the world could find out who the perpetrators of the 26/11 terror attacks in Mumbai were. If Ajmal too had died, Indian security agencies would have been able only to speculate where the attackers had come from and who had planned it.

The government of India has now honoured Omble with an Ashok Chakra (India's highest awarded for gallantry away from the battlefield) for his exemplary courage and bravery.

When the encounter at the Girgaum Chowpatty signal ended, the D B Marg police officers did not know that Omble had probably captured someone of international importance. As the police gathered around the injured Ajmal, the locals who had until then remained hidden in the bylanes, rushed out and started beating up Ajmal. The furious mob could have surely lynched Ajmal to death. Fortunately, wisdom prevailed and the police officers realised the importance of ensuring Ajmal's safety.

They immediately dispersed the crowd and put Ajmal into a police van and rushed him to the nearby Nair hospital. At the hospital, doctors, nurses and other hospital staff gathered around Ajmal to catch a glimpse of a *fidayeen*. They wondered how a young innocent-looking boy could kill so many innocent people, and still seem normal.

In the hospital, Ajmal was sad that he had been captured alive. At first, he begged the doctors to kill him, and then he said that he wanted to live, but requested the authorities not to let the news out that he was captured alive. "My handlers in Pakistan will kill my family if they know that I have been captured alive," Ajmal told a police officer.

After the doctors treated him for his wounds, the police officers took over. Ajmal told them everything about himself and why and how he had become a *fidayeen*.

2
The Plot

The emergency ward of Nair hospital wore an extremely busy look, as if some VIP had been admitted there. In a way, the patient being treated was no less than a VIP. A battery of doctors was pressed into service and the instructions to them were clear – ensure that Ajmal stays alive. Policemen checked the terrorist thoroughly for suicide pills or cyanide hidden on his person.

As news of Ajmal's arrest spread, a team of special police officers from the Mumbai crime branch was rushed to the hospital to question him. A few minutes past 2 am, the doctors were satisfied that Ajmal was in a condition to be questioned by the police.

Ajmal, who by now had realised that he had no choice but to cooperate with the police, started speaking. The first thing he told them that there were ten *fidayeens* who had attacked Mumbai. This information was passed on to the control room, which in turn relayed it to all the officers on the field.

The 20-year-old, also called 'Abu Mujahid', began narrating his story.

Hailing from a small village called Faridkot, on Kasur road in Dipalpur Tehsil of Okara District, in Punjab province of Pakistan, Ajmal was a class-four dropout. His family hailed from Chakmommedyar Chisti, Bashirpur Road in Dipalpur Tehsil, Okara District, Punjab, in Pakistan.

At an early age, his father Mohammad Amir had shifted to Faridkot. Ajmal's mother Noor-e-Elahi, a housewife, took care of Ajmal and his two brothers, and two sisters.

Ajmal studied in Faridkot, in the Government Primary School where open air classes were conducted till class four. After dropping out from school in 2000, Ajmal took up a few manual labour jobs for a few months in his village. Thereafter, he shifted to Lahore where his father and Uncle Gulam Rasool were residing and had a *chaat* selling business. Ajmal stayed there till 2005. During this period, he worked as a labourer for building contractors. He frequently returned to his native village.

In the latter part of 2005, Ajmal quarreled with his father, who had already shifted back to Faridkot, over his earnings. He was annoyed and left for Lahore and became an odd-job worker for a caterer there.

Soon, his employer shifted him to Sarai Alamgir, near Jhelum, where he owned a shop and had established his catering business. Ajmal worked there for a year. During this time, he came in contact with 22-year-old Muzaffar, a resident of Sarahad province, Pakistan.

Unhappy and unsatisfied with their work, Ajmal and Muzaffar decided that they had to do something more challenging to get more money and thrills. In 2006, they decided to commit a dacoity at an affluent businessman's house in Islamabad. Not satisfied with their current skills, Ajmal insisted that both of them acquire professional training in handling arms and ammunition before entering the world of crime. Subsequently they gave up their jobs and went to Rawalpindi.

They planned to get weapon's training at the camps of the Lashkar-e-Toiba (LeT). They had learnt that the LeT had an office in Rawalpindi. After staying in Rawalpindi for a few days they managed to locate the office.

At first, the office-bearers of the LeT dismissed the duo, but Ajmal and Muzzafar persisted. Impressed by their enthusiasm, the LeT ran a background check on them to find out if they were clean and then enrolled them in their preliminary training programme, Daura–e–Shufa. This training programme, Ajmal told the police, started at around the same time when Pakistan People's Party (PPP) leader Benazir Bhutto was assassinated in 2007.

TRAINING IN LeT CAMPS

Ajmal told the police that the first training programme lasted 21 days and was held at a camp in Muridke, in the Punjab Province of Pakistan. "This place was also called Markaz-e-Taiyyaba, Muridke," Ajmal told his interrogators. There were atleast 25 other Pakistani youth along with Ajmal at the camp. The camp turned out to be more of an orientation and conditioning camp.

Within two days after the Daura-e-Shufa ended, Ajmal was sent for another 21-day training camp in Manshera area of Pakistan Occupied Kashmir (POK). This training camp was also called Markaz-e-Taiyyaba, Bhattal. Ajmal and a group of 25-odd youths were given basic training in the handling of automatic rifles AK-47, Grinoff guns, M-16, Mycroft, and TT pistols.

After this camp wound up, Ajmal was asked to undergo a two month training programme called *khidmat* (hospitality) at the same camp. His job here was to help in the camp kitchen.

This marked the completion of the first phase of training. Immediately after this, the group was shifted to the hilly terrain of Cherapade region in Muzzaffarabad, in POK. Here, they had to undergo a two-and-a-half month training programme to handle arms and ammunition correctly. It was a level higher than the previous camp. The group was also taught to use gadgets like laptops, satellite phones, Global Positioning Systems (GPS), and a mariner's compass. They were also trained to use rocket launchers, grenades and other explosives.

At the camp, the youths were trained by *jehadis* who had returned after fighting in Jammu and Kashmir (J&K). "Those who fight in J&K are held in high esteem and are called 'Gazi'. It is considered a privilege to be trained by them," Ajmal told the police.

"I was taught the techniques and methods to be used during interrogation by the enemies in case I am caught," Ajmal said recalling that he was beaten and thrashed for several days during the training in order to be prepared for any kind of hostile interrogation.

They were also given maritime training to operate vessels and necessary gadgets to be used in marine operations.

Ajmal's high point came when he was given return tickets by his trainers after his training was over. "It meant that I had successfully cleared the training programmes and was selected for some *jehadi* activity," Ajmal reminisced.

After a week-long holiday, Ajmal was asked to come to a place in Azizabad, in Karachi. Here, he met Abdul Rehman, Chhota Abdul Rehman, Sohaib, Umair, Umar, Abu Akasa, Abu Ali, Ismail and Fahadulla – the rest of the ten-member *fidayeen* team.

At this camp, LeT commanders, Zaki and Kahafa, along with some locals living along the coast gave them logistic support including a hassle-free stay and food, and guarded their anonymity. Kahafa also gave them some books (translated from Urdu to Hindi) to improve their knowledge of Hindi.

All of them were divided into groups of two and each group was told to stay away from the others. Ajmal teamed up with Ismail Khan, who eventually became the leader of the entire team.

It was at this camp, that they were told that they had to carry out a *jehadi* activity in Mumbai, very soon.

TRAINING CAMP IN KARACHI

According to Ajmal, he was kept in a *haveli* in the Azizabad area of Karachi. During their stay here, Zaki Ur Rahman alias Chachu, the LeT commander, visited them at least three or four times. "Chachu showed us several video CDs containing provocative scenes from the Gujarat riots, Hyderabad Mecca Masjid blasts etc," Ajmal said.

A few days later, the five groups were each shown their specific targets on Google Earth as well as videos and maps of the target and the area around it. "We were also shown Budhwar Park in Cuffe Parade on Google Earth where we would be eventually getting off from the dinghy, on the day of the attack," Ajmal said. They were also shown how they could get to their respective targets from Budhwar Park.

"As the day of our departure neared, all ten of us were given new clothes and photographed for making fake college ID cards," Ajmal said.

On November 21 and 22, several top members of the LeT including Zaki Ur Rehman, Abu Hamza and Kahafa came to the *haveli* in Azizabad to bid farewell to the group.

FINAL JOURNEY

On November 23, 2008, the group of ten terrorists comprising Abdul Rehman, Chhota Abdul Rehman, Ismail, Ajmal, Sohaib, Umair, Umar, Abu Akasha, Fahadulla, and Abu Ali, were transported to an isolated creek in Azizabad. They got on to a small boat and set sail. After travelling for four nautical miles they got onto a much bigger launch – *Al Husseni.*

On board, all of them were given a bag each that contained eight grenades, one TT Pistol with two magazines, one improvised explosive device, an AK-47 assault rifle with six magazines, each containing atleast 32 bullets, a gas lighter, packets of dry fruits each weighing half kilogram, loose ammunitions, one mobile phone with an Indian SIM card, walkie-talkie sets, a few water bottles, and a college identity card of Arunodaya P G College, Teacher's Colony, Nagarabhave, Bangalore, India. "I got a card which had Samir Choudhary written on it," Ajmal recalled.

Ismail, who was in charge of the team, was given a satellite phone and a GPS system with the Mumbai-Karachi route stored on it.

Ajmal recalled that in the *Al Husseni* launch they were accompanied by five to six Pakistani nationals. After having sailed for a few hours, they hijacked an Indian fishing trawler – *MV Kuber*. "There were five Indian fishermen onboard," Ajmal said.

The ten *fidayeens* got onto *Kuber* and overpowered the crew. "The other Pakistani nationals who had accompanied us, stayed back on the *Al Husseni*, while we tied up the four Indian fishermen and transferred them to the *Husseni*," Ajmal said. The fifth Indian, the captain of *Kuber*, Amar Singh Tandel, was forced to navigate the trawler.

At this point, the *Al Husseni* sailed back towards Pakistan with the four Indian fishermen onboard. It is not yet clear what happened to them, but according to Ajmal they would have been killed. The *Kuber* sailed in the international waters towards Mumbai.

"A few hours later, Ismail called Chachu and asked him if they had slaughtered the *bakras*, when he got an affirmative, he killed Tandel and dumped his body in the engine room," Ajmal said, adding that after that Ismail took charge of the trawler and with the help of the GPS continued their journey.

The *fidayeens* had a three-day voyage and their jobs were defined in a diary (the diary was later recovered by the police). All of them had to do look-out duty in rotation. Some of them had to cook, while the others had to keep a close watch for Indian security ships.

"During the three days, we chanted verses from the Holy Quran to keep us motivated," Ajmal said. It was during this journey that they came to know about the targets of the other groups. Before this, they had been instructed not to disclose their targets to the others.

After an uneventful journey, the group reached near Mumbai around noon on November 26. "Ismail slowed the speed of the trawler, because we had instructions to carry out the operations in the night after nine," Ajmal said.

"At around half past six, Ismail signaled to all of us that it was time to go," Ajmal said. All ten of them offered a quick prayer and began the final leg of their journey. An inflatable dinghy (a small rubber speed boat) was taken out from one of the bags and pumped with air. A brand new engine of Yamaha-make was attached to it and lowered into the sea.

All ten of them sat in it, with Ismail taking control of the tiller. After a two-hour journey, at around 8.30 pm, their dinghy slowly moved towards the shore near fishermen colony in Cuffe Parade. "Eight of us jumped out of the dinghy in the shallow water and started walking towards the road in twos," Ajmal said.

Fahadulla and Chhota Abdul Rehman stayed back on the dinghy as they watched their other team members walk into Mumbai. They took the dinghy to Nariman Point and got off to go to the Oberoi Hotel. The dinghy was abandoned in the sea, but the *fidayeens* forgot to dispose of the most crucial evidence which later helped the Indian security agencies nail Pakistan – the satellite phone.

3
A Dangerous Mind Reveals All
(Ajmal's confession in his own words)

This is the statement Mohammad Ajmal Amir 'Kasab', 21, gave to the police soon after his arrest.

I have resided in Faridkot, Dipalpur Tehsil of Okara district, Suba Punjab state, Pakistan since my birth. I studied up to class four in a government school. After leaving school in 2000, I went to stay with my brother in Tohit Abad mohalla, near Yadgar Minar in Lahore. I worked as a labourer at various places till 2005, visiting my native place once in a while. In 2005, I had a quarrel with my father. I left home and went to Ali Hajveri Darbar in Lahore, where boys who run away from home are given shelter. The boys are sent to different places for employment.

One day a person named Shafiq came there and took me with him. He was from Zhelam and had a catering business. I started working for him for Rs 120 per day. Later, my salary was increased to Rs 200 per day. I worked with him till 2007. While working with Shafiq, I came in contact with one Muzzafar Lal Khan, 22. He was from Romaiya village in Alak district in Sarhad, Pakistan. Since we were not getting enough money, we decided to carry out robberies to make big money. So we left the job.

We went to Rawalpindi, where we rented a flat. Afzal had located a house for us to loot. We required some firearms for our mission. While we were in search of firearms, we saw some LeT stalls at Raja Bazaar in Rawalpindi on the day of Bakri-id. We then realised that even if we procured firearms, we would not be able to operate them. Therefore, we decided to join LeT for weapons training.

We reached the LeT office and told a person that we wanted to join LeT. He noted down our names and address and told us to come the next day. The next day, there was another person with him. He gave us Rs 200 and some receipts. Then he gave us the address of a place called Marqas Taiyyaba, Muridke, and told us to go there. It was an LeT training camp. We went to the place by bus. We showed the receipts at the gate of the camp. We were allowed inside. Then we were taken to the actual camp area.

Initially, we were selected for a 21-day training regimen called Daura-e-(Shufa). After that, our training started. The daily programme was as follows: 4.15 am – Wake-up call and thereafter Namaz; 8 am – Breakfast; 8.30 am to 10 am - Lecture on Hadis and Quran by Mufti Sayyed; 10 am to noon - Rest; Noon to 1 pm - Lunch break; 1 pm to 4 pm – Rest; 4 pm to 6 pm – PT, instructor: Fadulla;

6 pm to 8 pm – Namaz and other work; 8 pm to 9 pm – Dinner.

After Daura-e-Shufa, we were selected for another training programme called Daura Ama. This was also for 21 days. We were taken to Mansera in Buttal village, where we were trained in handling weapons.

The daily programme was as follows: 4.15 am to 5 am - Wake-up call and thereafter Namaz; 5 am to 6 am – PT, instructor: Abu Anas; 8 am – Breakfast; 8.30 am to 11.30 am – Weapons training, trainer: Abdul Rehman; weapons: AK-47, Green-O, SKS, Uzi gun, pistol, revolver; 11.30 am to Noon – Rest; Noon to 1 pm – Lunch break; 1 pm to 2 pm – Namaz; 2 pm to 4 pm – Rest; 4 pm to 6 pm – PT; 6 pm to 8 pm – Namaz and other work; 8 pm to 9 pm - Dinner.

After the training, we were told that we would begin the next stage of advanced training. But for that, we were told, we had to do some *khidmat* for two months (*khidmat* is a sort of service in the camp as per the trainee's liking). We agreed. After two months, I was allowed to go to meet my parents. I stayed with my parents for a month.

Then I went to an LeT camp in Shaiwainala, Muzaffarabad, for advanced training. We were taken to Chelabandi pahadi area for a training programme, called Daura Khas for three months. We learned to handle weapons, use hand grenades, rocket launchers, and mortar.

The daily programme was as follows: 4.15 am to 5 am – Wake-up call and thereafter Namaz; 5 am to 6 am – PT, instructor: Abu Mawiya; 8 am – Breakfast; 8.30 am to 11.30 am – Weapons training, handling of all weapons and firing practices with the weapons, training on handling hand grenade, rocket-launchers and mortars, Green-O, SKS, Uzi gun, pistol, revolver, trainer: Abu Mawiya; 11.30 am to 12 noon – Rest; Noon to 1 pm – Lunch break; 1 pm to 2 pm – Namaz; 2 pm to 4 pm – Weapons training and firing practice; lecture on Indian security agencies; 4 pm to 6 pm – PT; 6 pm to 8 pm – Namaz and other work; 8 pm to 9 pm – Dinner.

There were 32 trainees in the camp. Sixteen were selected for a confidential operation by one Zaki-ur-Rehman, alias Chacha, but three of them ran away from the camp.

Chacha sent the remaining 13 with a person called Kafa to the Muridke camp again.

At Muridke, we were taught swimming and made familiar with the life of fishermen at sea. We were given lectures on the working of Indian security agencies. We were shown clippings highlighting atrocities on Muslims in India. After the training, we were allowed to go to our native places. I stayed with my family for seven days. I then went to the LeT camp at Muzaffarabad. The 13 of us were present for training.

Then, on Zaki-ur-Rehman's instructions, Kafa took us to the Muridke camp. The training continued for a month. We were given lectures on India and its security agencies, including RAW. We were also trained to evade security personnel. We were instructed not to make phone calls to Pakistan after reaching India.

The names of the persons present for the training are: Mohd Azmal, alias Abu Muzahid, Ismail, alias Abu Umar, Abu Ali, Abu Akasha, Abu Umer, Abu Shoeb, Abdul Rehman (Bada), Abdul Rehman (Chhota), Fahadulla, and Abu Umar.

On September 15, Chacha selected 10 of us and formed five teams of two people each. Ismail and I formed a team; its codename was VTS. We were shown Azad Maidan in Mumbai on Google Earth's site on the internet. We were shown a film on VT railway station. The film showed commuters during rush hour. We were instructed to carry out firing during that time – between 7 am and 11 am, and between 7 pm and 11 pm. Then we were to take some people hostage, take them to the roof of some nearby building and contact Chacha, who would have given us numbers to contact media people and make demands. This was the strategy decided upon by our trainers. The date fixed for the operation was September 27. However, the operation was cancelled for some reason. We stayed in Karachi till November 23.

The other teams were: second team: Abu Aksha, Abu Umar; third team: Abdul Rehman (Bada), Abu Ali; fourth team: Abdul Rehman (Chotta), Afadulla; fifth team: Abu Shoeb, Abu Umer.

On November 23, the teams left from Azizabad in Karachi, along with Zaki-ur-Rehman and Kafa. We were taken to the nearby seashore. We boarded a launch. After travelling for 22 to 25 nautical miles we boarded a bigger launch. Again, after a journey of an hour, we boarded a ship, *Al Husseni*, in the deep sea. While boarding the ship, each of us was given a sack containing eight grenades, an AK-47 rifle, 200 cartridges, two magazines, and a cellphone.

Then we started towards the Indian coast. When we reached Indian waters, the crew members of *Al Husseni* hijacked an Indian launch. The crew of the launch was shifted to *Al Husseni.* We then boarded the launch. An Indian seaman was made to accompany us at gunpoint; he was made to bring us to the Indian coast. After a journey of three days, we reached near Mumbai's shore. While we were still some distance away from the shore, Ismail and Afadulla killed the Indian seaman (Tandel) in the basement of the launch. Then we boarded an inflatable dinghy and reached Badhwar Park jetty.

I then went along with Ismail to VT station by taxi. After reaching the hall of the station, we went to the toilet, took out the weapons from our sacks, loaded them, came out of the toilet and started firing indiscriminately at passengers. Suddenly, a police officer opened fire at us. We threw hand grenades towards him and also opened fire at him.

Then we went inside the railway station threatening the commuters and randomly firing at them. We then came out of the railway station searching for a building with a roof.

But we did not find one. Therefore, we entered a lane. We entered a building and went upstairs. On the third and fourth floors we searched for hostages but we found that the building was a hospital and not a residential building. We started to come down. That is when policemen started firing at us. We threw grenades at them.

While coming out of the hospital premises, we saw a police vehicle passing. We took shelter behind a bush. Another vehicle passed us and stopped some distance away. A police officer got off from the vehicle and started firing at us. A bullet hit my hand and my AK-47 fell out of my hand. When I bent to pick it up another bullet hit me on the same hand. Ismail opened fire at the officers in the vehicle. They got injured and firing from their side stopped. We waited for a while and went towards the vehicle.

There were three bodies in the vehicle. Ismail removed the bodies and drove the vehicle. I sat next to him. Some policemen tried to stop us. Ismail opened fire at them. The vehicle had a flat tyre near a big ground by the side of road. Ismail got down from the vehicle, stopped a car at gunpoint and removed the three lady passengers from the car. Since I was injured, Ismail carried me to the car. He then drove the car. We were stopped by policemen on the road near the seashore. Ismail fired at them, injuring some policemen. The police also opened fire at us. Ismail was injured in the firing. The police removed us from the vehicle and took us to the same hospital. In the hospital, I came to know that Ismail had succumbed to injuries.

My statement has been read to me and explained in Hindi, and it has been correctly recorded – Mohammad Ajmal Amir alias Kasab.

Source of Ajmal Kasab's confession – The confession was recorded by Maharashtra's Anti-Terrorism Squad (ATS) and provided by a source in the ATS.

4
Terror Travels By Sea

On the morning of November 26, the office of the Research and Analysis Wing (R&AW) intercepted a conversation on the Bangladesh border. The caller from across the border asked the person on the other end to activate ten SIM cards.

The intelligence agency failed to make sense of the conversation and dismissed it as a routine affair.

In hindsight, this proved to be a costly mistake because the caller was asking someone to activate the SIM cards which were eventually going to be used by the ten *fidayeens* who would be attacking Mumbai later in the evening, on that very day.

When the conversation was intercepted, the *fidayeens* were onboard a trawler in the Arabian Sea heading towards Mumbai.

After a journey of almost four days, the *Kuber* reached near the Mumbai coast.

It was around noon when they reached near the Mumbai coast. Ismail decided to slow the trawler because they had instructions to enter Mumbai after it was dark.

While they were slowly chugging towards their destination, one of them alerted the others about an Indian Navy patrol vessel approaching them quickly. The scared youngsters didn't know what to do and clutched their bags which had weapons. Ismail asked them to remain calm and warned them not to act in haste.

Officers on the patrol vessel gave a cursory glance towards the *Kuber* and dismissing it as any other fishing trawler and sailed past it. The *fidayeens* heaved a sigh of relief. But, they were rattled by the incident and did not want any more hiccups before they reached their destination.

At around 6.30 pm, when they were around four nautical miles away from the Mumbai shore, they embarked on their final journey. A rubbery dinghy was inflated and a new engine of Yamaha-make was attached to it.

All ten of them, slung their heavy backpacks, filled to the brim with weapons and ammunitions, over their shoulders and jumped onto the dinghy. In the melee, they forgot to dispose the satellite phone and left it on the *Kuber*. Their handlers had specifically instructed them to throw the phone in the sea so that the calls could not be traced.

It was a huge mistake, because Indian investigation agencies later recovered the phone from *Kuber* and traced the calls to Pakistan. Based on the handset number and other details, the investigators were able to track the phone and the conversations. It proved beyond doubt that Pakistan was involved in the attacks.

Ismail who was trained in maneuvering the dinghy started the engine and the *fidayeens* started towards Mumbai as the sun set. They recited religious hymns and songs to keep themselves motivated.

At around 8.30 pm, they approached the heavily illuminated sea front of Nariman Point and Cuffe Parade. Ismail took the dinghy directly towards the sea shore at Machchimar Colony situated opposite Budhwar Park in Cuffe Parade. The landing site was predetermined. As they reached the shore, eight of them got off, while two of them Abdul Rehman and Fahadulla stayed on board.

The sea shore was deserted because everyone was busy watching a one-day international cricket match between India and England. As they got off, a fisherwoman saw the *fidayeens*. She thought they were tourists who had come back after sailing in the water. She told them that it wasn't the spot for them to alight. The *fidayeens* asked her to mind her own business and walked past her.

Rehman and Fahadulla, took the dinghy towards Nariman Point as the eight *fidayeens* walked towards the road. Once on the main road, they divided into groups of two and went to their targets.

Ismail and his partner Mohammad Ajmal Amir alias Kasab, took a taxi to the CST railway station. Imran Babar and Nasir took a taxi towards Nariman House. Hafiz Arshad, Nazir, Javed, and Abu Ali took a taxi to the Taj Hotel.

Meanwhile, Rehman and Fahadulla had reached Nariman Point. They abandoned the dinghy and jumped on the tetrapods and started walking towards the Oberoi Hotel.

5
Leopold Café

A group of young wealthy businessmen were having their monthly kitty party at the Leopold Café. It was their regular hangout where the person who won that month would throw a party for the other members.

On November 26, it was the turn of 22-year-old Sandeep Kukreja (name changed on request) a diamond merchant. The twelve friends were sitting at their favourite table near the entrance of the café and enjoying their drinks, when a young man carrying a large backpack walked in. He seemed just like one of the many youngsters who hang out at the Café, which is very popular with foreign tourists.

The young man clad in cargo pants and black T-shirt, kept his backpack on the ground at the entrance, and glanced across the café. As if acting on some cue, he removed an AK-47 from his bag and pulled the trigger. A volley of bullets at the speed of 10 per second burst towards the table where Kukreja and his friends were sitting. Kukreja was among the first to be hit and collapsed on the floor the next instant.

Within moments, another gunman armed with a Kalashnikov assault rifle started firing. The gunmen just shot at random faces without targeting any particular individual. Almost everyone seated in the café, including several foreign nationals, were their victims.

Such was the ruthlessness that by the time they lifted their finger off the trigger, the gunmen had emptied two magazines (each magazine can have a maximum of 32 bullets) into the Café.

Nobody knew what was happening. Whether these were mad men on the loose, or if it was some kind of gang war related to drugs or the underworld, or even if it was only foreigners who were being targeted.

"A mad man is firing indiscriminately inside the Leopold Café," shouted a voice over the phone at the main control room of the Mumbai police in Crawford Market. The first reaction of the police was that it was probably a fight related to drugs. Alerts were sent to the police stations in Colaba.

The next call came within seconds, "Two armed men are firing randomly inside the Leopold Café, several foreigners injured." Again the reaction was that it was probably some kind of fight between rival gangs over drugs.

But the calls didn't stop. A senior police official who was on duty picked up one of the calls and listened attentively to the caller. Something told him that there was more to this event. The officer sent out a red alert to all senior officials and police stations across the city.

A few meters away from Leopold, Additional Commissioner of Police Hemant Nagrale was having dinner with his family in his residence above Colaba police station, when he heard gunfire. Nagrale immediately enquired if any news had reached the Colaba police station, but the policemen on duty dismissed the noise as crackers because India had won the cricket match.

After the second burst of gunfire, Nagrale knew that this was not the sound of crackers. Clad in his nightshirt, Nagrale grabbed his Glock 17 revolver and rushed towards Leopold Café.

When Nagrale reached the Café, he saw a bloodbath had taken place there with several foreigners among those who were injured or dead. Locals had already started taking the injured to the hospitals.

Meanwhile, the two gunmen after emptying the two magazines inside the Café and having fixed two fully loaded magazines into their gun, started walking towards the Taj Mahal Hotel. By the time they reached the back of the five-star hotel they had emptied the two magazines. The gunmen fired indiscriminately at anyone who was moving.

A police officer attached to the tourism police was patrolling near the Gateway of India in his vehicle when he heard the gunshots at Leopold Café and saw people running helter-skelter. The officer rushed towards the Café and took the lane the *fidayeens* had entered. Seeing the police vehicle, the gunmen fired a volley of bullets in the direction of the vehicle, three bullets pierced the officer's thigh. A bullet would have ripped apart the officer's abdomen, but the bullet hit the buckle of the service belt he was wearing.

Before barging into the Taj, the *fidayeens* managed to plant a deadly eight kilogram RDX bomb near the hotel. Fortunately, the bomb did not explode because the timer was not set properly and was later defused by the bomb squad. A similar bomb was planted by the other group of *fidayeens*, near Gokul Hotel in the lane behind the Taj. Even that bomb did not go off because of a problem with the timer. Had any of those two bombs exploded, then it would have caused unimaginable damage.

But, what followed was also of unimaginable magnitude.

6
The Taj Mahal

An elderly Sikh couple was strolling in the lane behind the Taj Mahal Hotel, an after-dinner routine that they were used to for several years. Since they often saw foreign and Indian tourists in and around the Taj, the couple did not find it strange when two youngsters clad in cargo pants and black T-shirts and heavily stacked haversacks walked past them towards the back door of the Taj.

While the duo waited for a moment outside the gate, the couple asked them if everything was alright and if they could be of any help. Looking at the elderly couple, one of the youngsters asked them to go home and close all doors and windows of their house. "*Yahan bahut hungama hone wala hai, ghar jao aur darwaaze khidkiyan bandh karlo* (There's going to be a lot of mayhem here, go home and close all the doors and windows)," they said in heavily Punjabi-accented Hindi.

Just as the couple turned to go back home, they heard a gunshot which broke the huge iron lock on the back door of the Taj. The couple knew something was horribly wrong when they then saw people running helter-skelter on the streets. As they rushed back to their apartment, they saw a couple of dead bodies lying in the lane which connects the Leopold Café and the Taj. Little did they know that they had just spoken with two *fidayeens* who along with eight others were going to create the kind of terror never seen or heard of anywhere in the world.

After wreaking havoc at Leopold Café, where nine people were killed and several innocents were injured, the *fidayeens* broke into India and Mumbai's pride – The Taj Mahal Hotel.

The terrorists immediately made their intentions absolutely clear. The moment they entered the premises of the hotel from the back, they were accosted by a security guard and his Labrador. An AK-47 bullet ripped through the body of the canine while another pierced the heart of the bodyguard. Before they could realise what was happening and find cover, two foreign nationals lazing near the pool were shot dead.

"It seems India has won the match," said a guest dining at a famous restaurant on the second floor of the heritage hotel. Such was the continuous burst of gunfire that most guests thought that the firecrackers were being lit since India won the match.

Some thought that guests at a wedding party at the Taj were celebrating noisily. They found it amusing that the crackers were set off inside the premises of the luxury hotel.

From the swimming pool, the *fidayeen* walked directly towards the lobby and started shooting at the guests in the lobby.

The guests who were caught unawares and were running for shelter, became easy targets for the remorseless *fidayeens.* A guest who flung himself on the floor and behind a pillar managed to catch a glimpse of the gunmen. "They had an eerie smile on their face when they were firing. It was as if they were getting an unusual satisfaction," the guest told the police after he was rescued a few hours later. By the time the *fidayeens* stopped firing, 20 people had been killed.

In retrospect, it was sheer luck that the *fidayeens* decided to move into the old Taj structure and not the new structure as there were close to 800 hundred guests in the new Taj.

In the heritage structure, two *fidayeens* were already waiting for the two gunmen who had entered from the backdoor. These two had entered the building from the side entrance even before the firing at Leopold began.

The four of them got together at the ground floor of the heritage hotel and took the elevator directly to the sixth floor (They had been instructed by their trainers to take a vantage position after the initial firing).

Meanwhile, the *fidayeens* who had taken control of the sixth floor started going from room to room to find out if they could take any hostages.

Sabina Sehgal Saikia, a consulting editor and resident food critic with *The Times of India*, was in Mumbai for a wedding reception but returned to her room at the Taj early, complaining of fatigue.

Trouble began soon after she got to her hotel room. Unable to understand what was happening, Sabina also sent a text message to the Public Relation Officer of the Taj.

What she said in her message was chilling, her message said that 'they' were inside the bathroom. Twenty minutes after she sent the message, one of the rooms on the sixth floor went up in flames. In all probability Sabina was in that room and had indicated through the message that the *fidayeens* were in her room.

General Manager of the Taj, Karambir Kang was attending an award function at the Taj Land's End Hotel in Bandra when the *fidayeens* entered Taj. Kang rushed to Taj as soon as he heard of the gunmen.

On his way to the hotel, he thought about his family – his wife and two children. Kang and his family had been living in a sixth floor suite in the heritage wing of the hotel. Ironically, Kang and his family were to move into a new apartment on January 1, 2009.

On reaching the hotel, Kang realised that he could not save his family as they were on the sixth floor where the *fidayeens* were hiding.

In an interview to a newspaper after the terror attacks,

Kang said that he knew his family was on the sixth floor, but thought they would be safe. But, the *fidayeens* had taken over the entire floor.

Kang's wife was speaking to him over the phone and he kept on reassuring her. But since he had to attend to all the guests trapped in the hotel, he could not keep talking to her. Kang tired to go to the sixth floor to help his family, but couldn't because the terrorists kept hurling grenades.

Over the next 60 hours, Kang and his staff helped evacuate guests from the hotel and saved approximately 700 lives. However, Kang's wife Niti and two sons Uday Singh and Samar Veer, aged 12 and five, died of asphyxiation in their room.

Karambir Kang was helping others even as his own family was in the line of fire. And yet, he did not let his personal tragedy overshadow his sense of duty.

Meanwhile, a team of four police officers from the Colaba police station who had reached the hotel by then were informed by the staff that the gunmen had taken the lift to the top floor. The officers needed to rush to the sixth floor and pin down the gunmen before any further damage could be caused.

Walking carefully so that they did not trip over the dozens of dead bodies lying on the floor, the policemen started climbing up the stairs.

It was eerily dark inside the hotel. The hotel management

had requested all guests to switch off the lights and mobile phones and lock the door from inside. They had also switched off all the lights in the corridors and even the central air conditioning system was put off.

The police team inched towards the steps expecting an attack from AK-56s. They were not sure how many *fidayeens* were in the hotel.

Shards of glass were strewn all over the floor. All over the floor, the blood of the innocent guests was slowly coagulating. This was an unnerving sight even for the Mumbai cops, who were considered specialists in gunning down gangsters.

The police officers later confessed that they knew they were no match for the *fidayeens*, who were armed with much sophisticated weapons. The professionally trained assassins were far too quick for the city policemen.

The police team heard a burst of gunfire when they reached the first floor. Minutes later a grenade exploded near them with a deafening impact. The cops were badly shaken. It was almost an hour since the start of the attack and they knew that they were up against highly trained *fidayeens*.

Assistant Police Inspector Deepak Dhawle and Sub-Inspector Nitin Kakde were soon joined by Deputy Commissioner of Police Vishwas Nagre Patil. He gained entry into the building using a flight of steps generally used as an emergency escape route.

The *fidayeens* resorted to intermittent fire with automatic weapons. Occasionally, they hurled a grenade. They also torched the dome abutting the sixth floor, where they had taken position. The wooden structures were now on fire which was spreading rapidly.

The smoke from the sixth floor had spread to the second floor. Visibility was poor since the entire floor was covered by thick black smoke.

A hotel staff directed the police party to a control room on the second floor. The idea was to find the *fidayeens* on CCTV before closing in on them.

Even before officers of the Mumbai police could get into the room, they were greeted with another burst of gunfire. The bullets hit a State Reserve Police Force (SRPF) guard, who died on the spot. Shaken by the loss, the police tried to return the fire with their service revolvers. It was also a message to the *fidayeens* that the police was nearby and challenging them.

The police team had to withdraw at around 3.30 am. They were unable to breathe due to the toxic smoke, which had enveloped four floors.

The naval marine commandos or Marcos as they are called, had taken position in the building by 2.20 am. Initially, they covered the police teams engaged to rescue high profile guests. The 30-odd Marcos then divided into three groups and spread across the hotel. They were assigned the task to contact the *fidayeens*.

A naval commander who led the Marcos confessed the following day (November 27) that the *fidayeens* knew the hotel better than they did. Later, the highly trained commandos closed in on one of the *fidayeens* and killed him. The commandos recovered a haversack containing a huge cache of ammunition, several credit cards and six hand grenades. Significant quantities of dry fruits were found in the bag too.

OPERATION TORNADO

The National Security Guard (NSG) took over operations at around 9 am on November 27, almost 10 hours after the *fidayeens* broke into the hotel. Their first task was to take charge of the second floor, which was secured by the Marcos in the wee hours of the morning.

An NSG unit was assigned the task to establish contact (establishing contact in military terms is sighting where the enemy is and engaging him in cross-firing) while another team was deployed to rescue guests. It was a difficult task needing door-to-door intervention and the guests who had locked themselves in were too afraid to open the door to anyone. In most cases, the NSG had to break the doors open with mild explosives to rescue the guests hiding in the 450-odd rooms.

The NSG began sanitising and cleansing each floor and each room as they closed in on the *fidayeens*. By Friday afternoon, the NSG had announced the elimination of two of the four fidayeens.

On Friday evening, after having cornered the two *fidayeens* on the first and second floor, the NSG began its final assault to flush the two *fidayeens* out. Teams of commandos attacked the two floors from all sides. Within a few hours the *fidayeen* on the second floor was killed after the NSG attacked him with MP5 guns and grenades.

The last *fidayeen* was injured, but trying to hold on as long as possible. He was holed up on the first floor and would fire in small bursts indicating that he still had some ammunition with him.

At daybreak on Saturday, it was just a matter of time before the last of the four *fidayeens* was eliminated. A team of NSG commandos attacked a hall situated on the first floor. This hall had been converted into a mini control room by the *fidayeens*. All their equipment, weapons and belongings were there.

In a two-pronged attack, the commandos hurled grenades inside the hall from outside the hotel and another team targeted the entrance of the hall. The *fidayeen* was injured in a grenade attack. The commandos then stormed the hall after first hurling a grenade and then firing inside the hall.

At around 8 am on Saturday morning, the last of the ten *fidayeens* who had wreaked havoc in Mumbai for three days was eliminated.

In a gesture which was one of the most defining moments of the 26/11 terror attacks, the NSG commandos threw the *fidayeen's* body out of the ground floor window rather than taking him out from the exit. The gesture was a clear message to the terrorists, not to mess with India anymore.

MAJOR SANDEEP UNNIKRISHNAN

One of the NSG teams, the 51 Special Action Group (SAG) was headed by Major Sandeep Unnikrishnan who was incharge of establishing contact with the *fidayeens.*

"Do not come up, I will handle them," Unnikrishnan told his team members before he was killed in combat by the *fidayeens.*

While Unnikrishnan and his team had engaged the *fidayeens* in a fierce gun battle a commando had been injured. Unnikrishnan arranged for his evacuation and started chasing the terrorists himself. The terrorists escaped to another floor of the hotel and during the chase Unnikrishnan was shot at by the *fidayeens.* He was seriously injured and soon succumbed to his injuries.

Hailing his efforts, NSG Director General J K Dutt said that Major Sandeep Unnikrishnan played a stellar role in eliminating the terrorists.

A young, ambitious, talented, and brave man, Unnikrishnan joined the National Defence Academy in 1994 and was commissioned as Second Lieutenant to the Bihar 7th Regiment in 1999.

After serving the Indian Army in different locations in

Jammu & Kashmir to counter insurgencies, he was selected to join the National Security Guards. On completion of training, he was deputed to the NSG on January 20, 2007 and participated in various operations conducted by the elite force.

Major Unnikrishnan was the commander of 51 SAG which was deployed in the operation Black Tornado at Taj Mahal Hotel. Thirty-one-year-old Major Sandeep is the only son of retired ISRO officer K. Unnikrishnan, who is settled in Bengaluru.

7
The Oberoi

After offloading the eight *fidayeens* at the Machchimar Colony at Cuffe Parade, two *fidayeens* onboard the black dinghy turned once again towards the sea. Their job was to get to the Land's End at Nariman Point as soon as possible and attack the Trident and Oberoi Hotel.

Abdul Rehman and Fahadulla started the Yamaha engine attached to the dingy as they hurriedly turned back while their eight team members walked towards the main road. They had just survived a major scare – a fisherwoman sitting on her boat near the shore had asked them what they were doing there at that time of the day. They asked her to mind her own business and walked away.

Rehman and Fahadulla were hoping that she would not raise an alarm because they still had about ten minutes in the water before they reached their destination.

It was sultry while they were trying to maneuver their dinghy through the boats and trawlers anchored near the seashore. Even though it was night, the bright lights along the sea front of Cuffe Parade and Nariman Point were more than enough for navigation.

The Yamaha engine slowly chugged to a halt near the tetrapods at the Land's End at Nariman Point. The duo was dressed in cargo pants and black T-shirts, which made them look like tourists. Anxious to get off the dinghy quickly, Rehman and Fahadulla strapped on their heavy backpacks and jumped on the tetrapods. They left the dinghy floating in the water, not realising that they had committed a very serious mistake, which would later prove to be very costly. None of the ten *fidayeens,* including Rehman and Fahadulla, thought about disposing the satellite phone which they had brought from Karachi. They had instructions to throw the phone in the water as soon as they reached Mumbai and interact via local mobile phones.

The dinghy and the satellite phone were later recovered by the police, which clearly proved that the perpetrators of 26/11 had indeed come from Pakistan. The satellite phone record and the data recovered from it proved to be a huge bonus for the police.

Immediately after jumping from the dinghy to the tetrapods, the duo started walking towards the five-star hotels which are considered to be jewels in the Queen's Necklace. The usually crowded promenade was relatively empty. A day and night cricket match between India and England had drawn everyone home.

The duo walked towards the entrance of the Trident,

which is the older and taller of the two hotels. They had chosen on this hotel, because the entrance of the Oberoi which is a new building is rather confusing – one has to get into an elevator at ground level to reach the lobby of the hotel.

After they walked past the entrance and reached the lobby of the Trident, they took out their AK-47 assault rifles and opened fire. Their first target was the reception desk of the hotel, two staff members were severely injured.

Before the hotel staff and the guests sitting in the lobby could realise what was happening, the two gunmen had rushed towards the lobby of the Oberoi.

It was another weeknight at Tiffin and Kandhar – the two restaurants situated in the lobby and first floor of the Oberoi. Diners in these restaurants heard the initial gunshots from the lobby and dismissed it to be firecrackers as the Indian cricket team had won the match.

Almost all the tables in Tiffin were occupied, while some people had just finished dinner, some had just settled in and were perusing the menu. Some were half-way through their drinks and enjoying the evening.

Within moments all this changed as death stared them in the face. Standing at the entrance to the famous restaurant, the two gunmen – Rehman and Fahadulla – held their rifles as if it were nothing more than a guitar, and pressed the trigger of their Kalashnikov rifles and sprayed bullets.

Before anyone could react, people were on the floor, dead.

Screams of terror drowned in the gunfire. Within minutes, the two magazines containing 32 bullets each were empty as the two gunmen ran up the stairs towards Kandhar restaurant.

As if time had stopped at Tiffin – the tables still had half-eaten food, glasses filled with wine and champagne and menu cards across the table as if someone was yet to order food. But there were no guests – they were lying dead on the floor. Those who managed to duck in time were still kneeling down, unable to come to terms with what they had just witnessed.

"It was like a scene from a Hollywood movie," said a guest who managed to take cover in time. But for those who survived, their misery had just begun. The enormity of the situation dawned after they saw the number of people lying dead on the floor and the entire floor covered with blood.

A forensic expert who later visited Tiffin said that such was the precision of the shots that not a single bullet had hit the walls or the ceiling of the restaurant. "Which means they were trained to shoot at head-level and waist-level," the expert said.

Even before anyone could get up, the sounds of another round of gunfire was heard from the first floor. Rehman and Fahadulla had by then reached Kandhar and had shot the diners. Unlike Tiffin, Kandhar has just one door for entering and exiting. Taking advantage of this, the *fidayeens* stood at the door and opened fire.

Kandhar, a popular meeting place for corporate honchos and business tycoons, was packed to capacity when the *fidayeens* got there Even though the diners and staff had heard the gunshots, before they could react and take cover, the *fidayeens* had blocked the exit.

Two more magazines were emptied by the ruthless gunmen at this restaurant. Within minutes, the restaurant was turned into a chamber of death. Those who managed to take cover were later escorted to safety through the backdoor in the kitchen by the hotel staff.

With the success of the first part of their operation, the *fidayeens* launched the second phase. The second phase involved taking as many hostages as possible and a vantage position in the hotel.

Atleast a dozen people were taken hostage by the gunmen and taken to the 19th floor of the Oberoi Hotel.

Meanwhile, the local police had been alerted by the hotel staff and the first batch of police officers entered the hotel. Their top priority was to rescue as many people as possible and rush the injured to the hospital.

On seeing the magnitude of the attacks, the .303 rifle-wielding police immediately knew that they were no match for the sophisticated assault rifles of the *fidayeens.* Also, with news pouring in from other parts of the city that were under attack, the cops knew that this was nothing like any crime they had ever encountered before. This was a series of well coordinated terror attacks.

The police decided to carry on with their rescue operation, in the midst of gunfire and grenade explosions. After the initial burst of shots, there was a pause, probably because the *fidayeens* had taken hostages and were looking for a safe vantage point. Taking advantage of this, the police started rescuing people from the hotel.

Guests stuck on the higher floors of the Trident and the Oberoi were instructed by the hotel staff to stay indoors and await further instructions.

While, the rescue operation was on, additional commissioner of police of the Anti-Terrorism Squad (ATS) of Maharashtra, Param Bir Singh, reached the Oberoi Hotel and took charge of the situation. He along with a few officers quickly summed up the situation and figured that the *fidayeens* were hiding on the higher floors in the Oberoi and could have hostages with them.

The first thing they did was to seal all the exits in the hotels to ensure that the *fidayeens* couldn't escape. The *fidayeens* had reached the 19th floor along with the hostages and once again opened fire. They had the advantage of being higher up and also the fact that the entire hotel was blacked out.

Teams of the Rapid Action Force (RAF), Marine Commandos (Marcos) and the Army reached the hotel in quick succession. The Marcos tried to barge their way into the hotel, but each time the Marcos would make an attempt to go up, they would be attacked by bullets and grenades.

The commandos of the elite National Security Guards (NSG) finally arrived early on Thursday morning. They were greeted with cheering and applause from the crowd that had gathered outside the Oberoi. The sight of the commandos brought relief to the people following the overnight drama.

The NSG Major General R K Hooda arrived at the scene and was briefed by Param Bir Singh about the location of the *fidayeens* and how many hostages they probably had.

Hooda briefed the anxious press and media persons. "Our efforts are to bring back all the people safely. The NSG are trained to handle the situation and they are the best at it. So have faith in them. We cannot quantify the time. It is a deliberate operation," Hooda said to the electronic media.

After this 250-300 armed commandos from the NSG started a frontal attack on the *fidayeens* holed up in the luxury hotel. In a tactical move, while a team of commandos entered the hotel from the top floor and took charge of the 21st floor, another decided to plant themselves in the NCPA apartments situated exactly opposite the new wing.

The NSG took over rooms of atleast 10 apartments facing the Oberoi Hotel. From here the NSG snipers got a clear view of the *fidayeens* who were holed up on the 19th floor.

The stand-off continued for the entire day on Thursday. On one hand, the NSG engaged the *fidayeens* in a gun battle, and on the other hand they started cleansing and sanitizing the hotel premises.

Since there was still no clarity on the number of gunmen inside the hotel, the NSG could not afford to take any chances. They had to check each and every room in the hotel and ensure that the guests were rescued safely while ensuring that they did not fall prey to any booby traps laid by the *fidayeens*.

Finally, after almost 45-hours of intense gun battle, the two *fidayeens* came in the range of the NSG commandos who were in the NCPA apartments. A shot from the MP5 sub machine gun from one of the NSG snipers pierced through the body of Rehman. This was followed by a desperate exchange of fire between Fahadulla and the NSG. Fahadulla was finally felled on Friday morning.

After a thorough check and intensive cleansing of the hotel, Hooda came out and declared that the Oberoi had been taken.

8
The Nariman House

Before November 26, 2008, most people in Mumbai did not even know of its existence. It would be fair to say that 26/11 gave birth to a new address in Mumbai – The Nariman House, home to members of the orthodox Jewish group, Chabad Lubavitch.

On the night of 26/11 when news started pouring in of the mayhem at Leopold café, Taj Mahal Hotel, the Oberoi Hotel and CST station, everyone knew the importance of these places. But, why was Nariman House being attacked? Nobody knew. In fact, a number of policemen also did not know of its existence.

Everyone's first reaction to this information was that Nariman House was probably a building in the elite Nariman Point area and was therefore attacked by the *fidayeens*.

But the attackers and their handlers back in Pakistan knew each and every detail of this place. Nariman House was deliberately made a target because the radical Islamic organizations in Pakistan wanted to send out a strong message to the Jews.

The two *fidayeens* – Imran Babar and Nasir – who were given the job of attacking Nariman House were given clear instructions that even if the other operations failed, the Nariman House operation should not fail under any circumstance. The duo was warned that they should not take any chances and should ensure that they do not alert anybody before gaining entry into Nariman House.

Both Babar and Nasir had gotten off at Machchimar Colony at Cuffe Parade along with the six other *fidayeens*. It is not yet clear whether they took a taxi to Nariman House or if they walked there. While, preliminary investigations have revealed that the duo took a taxi from the Machchimar Colony. The Global Positioning System (GPS) recovered from the slain *fidayeens* indicates that they had plans to walk the distance.

Whether they went by taxi or walking, it took them more than an hour to reach Nariman House which is a mere ten minutes away from the Machchimar Colony. Anybody aware of the exact topography of the area can reach Nariman House in ten minutes from Budhwar Park, where the *fidayeens* got off the dinghy.

On reaching the place, the *fidayeens* started their attack by hurling a grenade at a petrol pump situated near the synagogue. They then entered Nariman House and started shooting.

The Holtzberg family, including the Rabbi and his wife Rivika had just finished dinner and had returned to their rooms for the day, when they heard gunshots.

The two gunmen started climbing up the stairs shooting at whatever and whoever came their way.

Sandra Samuel, nanny at the Nariman House was in the kitchen for the post-dinner cleaning up. It was just like another day, with the guests returning to their rooms after dinner and the Rabbi and his wife returning to their rooms for the night prayers.

She heard a loud explosion and a series of sounds which sounded like fire crackers. She felt as if the noise came from within the premises of Nariman House. It was quite strange and she stepped out of the kitchen to check. Just as she stepped out, she heard another round of firecrackers. Within moments, two shadows emerged from the darkness. Sandra gathered that something was wrong, because the shadows were heavily armed.

Instinctively, Sandra rushed back into the kitchen and took cover behind a huge iron cupboard. The two armed men heard noise in the kitchen and shot inside the kitchen.

Recounting her feeling of helplessness while she lay motionless behind the cupboard, Sandra later told a television news channel, "I have nightmares about this. Me sitting behind the cupboard and another worker near the fridge. We wanted to do something, but couldn't do anything."

"After several hours, when the firing and bombings stopped for a while, I gathered some courage to step out of the kitchen. As I stepped out I saw that the entire building was severely bombed. It was like a war-affected building," Sandra told the news channel.

Her first thoughts went for Baby Moshe, was he safe? wondered Sandra as she went looking for him. "My first thought was always for the baby.... Even today, I am thinking I should have sent the baby and done something for the Rabbi and his wife," Samuel told CNN in an interview a few days after the attacks.

As she was climbing the stairs, she heard faint cries of the baby, her heart sank and her stomach felt heavy. When she ran upstairs, she saw Baby Moshe, standing next to her mother, his clothes soaked in blood and was crying for Ima (mother). "When Moshe saw me he started crying even louder and called out to me," Sandra recalled.

Her first instinct was to grab the baby and run to safety. "I was thinking just take the baby and run. Just then the firing resumed, I just picked up the baby and ran," Sandra told CNN.

Samuel grabbed Moshe in her arms as *fidayeens* once again resumed the firing and ran out of the Chabad House, not looking back even once. As she ran out, the police immediately took her and Moshe to safety.

Six Jews, including Rabbi Gavriel Holtzberg and his wife Rivika, were killed during the siege of Nariman House where the Jewish couple ran a cultural and outreach centre for the Chabad-Lubavitch movement.

On the day of the attack, the Holtzbergs were hosting a small group in the ultra-Orthodox centre. An unarmed Indian guard sat outside as five Jewish travellers dropped in for afternoon prayers, a kosher meal at the Holtzbergs' table, and a bed for the night.

Yocheved Orpaz, a 60-year-old Israeli, was en route to join her family on an Indian vacation. Rabbi Aryeh Leibish Teitelbaum, a 37-year-old American resident of Israel, and his friend Bentzion Chroman, 28, a dual US-Israeli citizen, were in India as part of their international work supervising the preparation of kosher food.

They were joined by David Bialka, a 52-year-old diamond trader and a frequent guest at the centre, on his business travels, and Norma Shvarzblat Rabinovich, a 50-year-old Mexican Jew visiting India on her way to start a new life in Israel.

Bialka had just fallen asleep and was roused by an explosion. He squeezed through a small fifth-floor bathroom window and shimmied down water pipes, hopping from one air-conditioning unit to another until he reached the ground.

Aroused by the commotion, an angry crowd had already gathered outside the building and mistook Bialka for a militant. They attacked him and took him to the police station. At the police station, encounter specialist Vijay

Salaskar (who was later killed near Cama Hospital) questioned him and cleared him.

Neighbours heard two blood-curdling screams, one from a man and the other from a woman, and gathered outside the centre. A *fidayeen* tossed out a grenade, killing one person in the crowd.

By the time security officer Raz and another armed Israeli arrived, the crowd was so agitated that it chased them to the police station too. They were detained for hours.

Israelis and Indians say it took the police long to respond to calls about the terrorists in Nariman house. Kamaljeet Singh, who witnessed the grenade explosion, said he rushed to a police station and then to a nearby naval base, but officers told him they had no permission from the higher-ups to act.

The house was quiet the next morning, until nanny Sandra Samuel heard Moshe's cries. Samuel picked up the boy and fled the building. Tragically, Moshe was orphaned on the very day he turned two. The bodies of Moshe's parents were found by the commandos of the NSG who stormed Nariman House after killing the two *fidayeens*.

According to unconfirmed reports, on Thursday afternoon the rabbi's cell phone rang. A *fidayeen* answered in Urdu. Rabbi Levi Shemtov was calling from Washington, trying desperately to reach his Chabad-Lubavitch colleague. The *fidayeen* could not speak English, so the rabbi found an interpreter and dialed again.

Without identifying a cause or spelling out demands, the *fidayeen* promised to free his captives if he got what he wanted. He identified himself as Imran Babar, age 25, and said all the hostages were OK. Shemtov promised to put Babar in touch with Indian authorities. But efforts to patch an Indian police official into a subsequent call failed.

Babar reportedly spoke to a Hindi news channel as well. Even though he did not put forth any specific demands, he justified his attacks as an answer to the atrocities committed on Muslims in Gujarat and Jammu and Kashmir.

After this, all efforts to get in touch with the *fidayeens* were in vain.

OPERATION BLACK THUNDER

The NSG reached Nariman House on Thursday afternoon and took charge of the situation. Before the NSG arrived, a 58-year-old Assistant Commissioner of Police Isaque Bagwan along with a few constables and armed only with half a dozen .303 rifles had been keeping an eye on Nariman House for 18 hours.

The NSG's job was made easy because Bagwan with the help of locals had already evacuated the 500-odd families staying in the crowded area. The NSG snipers took vantage positions in all the buildings surrounding the Nariman House and operation Black Thunder began.

The operation which lasted for close to 50-hours was full

of high drama with NSG commandos engaging in a full-on gun battle with the *fidayeens*. The sight of helicopters air-dropping NSG commandos on the terraces of buildings adjacent to Nariman House is probably among the most unforgettable moments of the terror attacks. NSG commando Gajendra Singh lost his life when a bullet fired by the *fidayeens* pierced his heart.

By Friday night the NSG, amidst chants and patriotic slogans from the locals, declared that Nariman House was taken after their snipers barged into the six-storeyed building and killed the two gunmen.

One of the most distressing events was the telephonic conversation intercepted by Indian intelligence agencies in which the Pakistan-based handlers of the *fidayeens* told them to kill the Jews so that tensions between India and Israel would escalate.

9
CST – Cama Hospital

Making their way into the railway station on the night of November 26, mingling with the crowd of long-distance commuters were two youngsters who had gotten off a taxi near Chhatrapati Shivaji Terminus (CST). Once inside the terminus for long-distance trains, the duo scanned the area looking for an isolated corner where they could stop for a moment. Their eyes darted from one corner of the premise to the other, but they couldn't find a place that wasn't crowded.

The terminus was abuzz with hundreds of commuters and passengers waiting for their trains. The duo, Ismail Khan and Mohammad Ajmal Amir alias Kasab, too were waiting in the crowd but they didn't have to catch any train, they had different plans.

Ismail looked at the gent's toilet at the far end of the platform adjacent to the parcel office. Asking Ajmal to follow him, Ismail walked into the toilet. Both of them freshened up as if they were about to start on a journey.

They removed two fully loaded AK-47 rifles from their backpacks, flung the bags over their shoulders and walked out of the toilet. They took positions close to each other in a manner reminiscent of army personnel and started shooting the travellers.

As the sounds of indiscriminate firing echoed in the heritage structure of the CST station, people caught unawares started running for cover. Those in the sight of the killers collapsed to the floor.

Iqbal Ansari, a 47-year-old man from Aurangabad, who was waiting for his train, tripped and fell down. He lay motionless on the floor as though he were dead. From the corner of his eye he tried to catch a glimpse of the gunmen. What he saw sent a chill down his spine.

"The younger of the two gunmen was firing at innocents as if he was watering plants, but even more chilling was the eerie smile he had on his face and a glint in his eye while he was shooting," Ansari remembers. "It was as if a child had finally got a toy which he had wanted for a long time. It was the scariest thing I have ever seen and that image has been etched in my memory forever," he said.

Their finger never left the trigger of their Kalashnikovs as the *fidayeens* walked across the platform shooting anything and everything that moved.

Police inspector Shashank Shinde, posted at the CST railway police station had finished his shift at 9 pm but instead of heading home he had decided to stay back to watch the ensuing cricket match between India and England. This decision, in retrospect, proved fatal for Shinde.

Just as the match got over at around 9.45 pm, Shinde and his colleagues heard gunshots and a loud explosion within the station premises. As they rushed out of their police station, situated between the local train terminus and the main line train terminus, they saw people running for cover.

Looking at the wounds of the injured, Shinde knew that the gunmen were lethally armed. Clutching his service revolver, Shinde took cover behind a pillar and started exchanging fire with the two.

Ismail who had by then emptied his second magazine, took cover behind an iron pillar to load a fresh magazine. Shinde seized the opportunity and lunged towards Ismail to catch him before he could load his rifle. But before Shinde could lay his hands on Ismail, a volley of bullets fired by Ajmal pierced Shinde's body and felled him.

Constable Ambadas Pawar, attached to the protection branch of the Mumbai police, had just got off the local train at the CST railway station. He was on night duty and was headed towards his office situated on the Vaju Kotak Marg in Ballard Pier, a ten minute walk from CST.

Seeing people running and screaming, Pawar instantly knew something was wrong. He rushed in the direction of the gunfire. Taking cover and ensuring that he could not be seen by the gunmen, Pawar hid behind a wall. A railway police constable had taken position there and was attempting to fire from his .303 rifle. Pawar stood behind him.

However, after a couple of rounds the gun jammed and the constable was unable to shoot. Seeing his predicament Pawar crawled close to him and asked him to hand over the gun. The constable hesitated, Pawar told him that he was also a constable with the crime branch and was trained in handling weapons. The constable handed him the gun and took cover behind the wall.

Pawar instantly undid the jam and took position. From the place where Pawar was in position, he had a clear view of Ajmal. Pawar waited patiently for Ajmal to come within range, but he did not realise that Ismail had crept up behind him. This time it was Ismail's turn to return the favour as he fired a shot at Pawar. The bullet pierced Pawar's head from behind, killing him instantly.

In spite of this, the brave railway policemen armed with archaic .303 rifles, also known as the *danda* (stick) gun, and wooden sticks continued to engage the *fidayeens* and chase them. This quick retaliation by the railway cops rattled the *fidayeens* because neither were they prepared for it, nor were they trained to tackle the retaliatory onslaught by the railway police.

The flustered *fidayeens* could not take any hostages and had to beat a hasty retreat from the station. The remorseless duo walked right across to the local train terminus, which was deserted by now. Looking for an exit they entered the subway. Realising that they might get trapped inside it, they climbed back on to the platform and started looking for a vantage position.

At the end of platform number 1 they saw stairs and thought it would take them to a place from where they could get a clear view. When they climbed the bridge they realised that it was a footover bridge to get to the other platforms and across the road. With the railway police personnel on their heels, the duo decided to leave the railway premises.

As they got off the footover bridge, they entered Anjuman lane between *The Times of India* building and the Anjuman-e-Islam school. Desperate to look for cover and seek refuge, the duo tried to open the doors of cars that were parked in the lane. When they did not succeed, they walked into the lane which was dark.

Not sure where they were headed, the gunmen fired randomly while walking. A kid who lived in the nearby hutments, was answering nature's call, and was shot at. The startled kid fell to the ground motionless as though he had died, although the bullet had just grazed his shoulder. As soon as the gunmen walked past him, the kid jumped the wall and disappeared into the hutments.

Ismail and Ajmal did not know where they were going but knew that they were running out of time and had to look for a tall building where they could seek refuge. They reached the back door of Cama Hospital. Not knowing that it was a hospital, they entered the six-storeyed annex building and killed two security personnel at the entrance.

An eerie silence crept through the hospital as everyone realised that the gunmen had entered the building. The hospital staff did a commendable job of calming the patients and herding them to safety. Their worst nightmare – there were at least 60 newborn babies in the hospital. If the babies started crying, it would give away their location. The doctors and nurses on-duty instructed the mothers to suckle the young ones for as long as possible so that they did not get scared by the gunshots.

Ismail and Ajmal started walking up the stairs, it was dark as all the lights had been switched off. On the fifth floor, 52-year-old Harishchandra Shrivardhankar was trying to take cover in one of the rooms when he came face-to-face with the terrorists.

Left with no choice, Shrivardhankar decided to fight back rather become a helpless victim. Within a fraction of a second, Shrivardhankar pounced on Ismail. A startled Ismail retaliated by slashing his throat and hitting him with the AK-47.

Shrivardhankar, a resident of Kalyan, a township near Mumbai, sustained life-threatening wounds. He suffered two gashes on neck and two bullets in the back, but he put up a valiant fight. He managed to knee the attacking *fidayeen* in the groin and hit him in the head with a carry bag.

Shrivardhankar's attack shocked Ismail and Ajmal as they ran up the stairs on the sixth floor and then on the terrace where they decided to rest for a while. Little did they know that there were 25 pairs of anxious eyes watching them as they rested in one corner of the terrace.

10
Karkare, Kamte & Salaskar Encounter

Chief of the Anti-Terrorism Squad (ATS) of the Maharashtra police, Hemant Karkare was having dinner with his family at his residence on the night of November 26, when the mayhem started. A man of few but precise words, Karkare would never bring home his work, but recently he had been perturbed following the investigations into the Malegaon (a Muslim dominated town north of Mumbai) bomb blasts.

A few hours before he sat for dinner at his Dadar residence, Karkare had met the then Home Minister R R Patil and urged Patil to transfer him out of the ATS.

In the days immediately preceding the 26/11 attacks, Karkare was under a lot of fire from the Hindutva groups in the country. Because Karkare and his ATS had for the first time unearthed 'Hindu Terrorism' while investigating the September 29, Malegaon bomb blasts.

The 53-year-old IPS officer from the 1982 batch of police officers was hurt by the baseless allegations leveled against him by the radical Hindutva groups, because the ATS had arrested a serving lieutenant colonel of the Indian Army, a Sadhvi (a lady hermit) and a self-proclaimed godman for their alleged role in the Malegaon bomb blasts. Karkare had privately told his superiors that he was extremely upset with allegations that his actions were politically motivated.

Just as he finished dinner, Karkare got a call from the police control room informing him about gunfights in South Mumbai. A few calls later, it was clear that this was no ordinary fight between Mumbai's criminal gangs.

Karkare immediately got into the vehicle and rushed to South Mumbai. As he reached JJ flyover, he received news that two gunmen had entered Cama Hospital. The local police had barricaded the road near Haj House and no vehicles were allowed beyond that point. Karkare alighted from his vehicle near Haj House and was briefed about the latest developments by a senior officer from the ATS.

A media contingent gathered near the Haj House tried to speak to him regarding the attack. In spite of the prevailing circumstance, the ever-polite Karkare said that he would speak to them later. "It seems to be a terror attack. I will finish the job and then speak to you," were his last words to the media before he turned and started walking towards the CST station.

His walk towards CST station, which was captured by some TV news channels, is etched in everyone's memory.

He wore the bullet-proof jacket and a helmet while he was being briefed.

Meanwhile, Additional Commissioner of Police Ashok Kamte had also reached South Mumbai. A brilliant marksman and a dynamic officer, Kamte was in charge of the eastern suburbs of Mumbai. He was attending a function in Chembur when his bodyguard alerted him about the firing in South Mumbai.

Kamte made a few phone calls and immediately knew that the situation was serious. Being in charge of the eastern suburbs Kamte could have stayed back and ensured that law and order in the eastern suburbs stayed under control. But going beyond the call of his duty, Kamte decided to rush to South Mumbai. Before leaving, he instructed his deputy to ensure that there were no untoward incidents in the eastern suburbs. He also instructed his subordinates to take special precautions in areas surrounding the highly sensitive Bhabha Atomic Research Centre and Rashtriya Chemical Fertilizers.

Taking the Mumbai Port Trust road, Kamte reached the GPO junction outside CST station. The local police had barricaded the road at the junction and were not allowing any vehicles beyond that point.

The control room informed Kamte that the two gunmen had entered Cama Hospital. Kamte decided to walk the distance. He grabbed his AK-47 and started walking towards the Cama hospital along with his bodyguard.

Mumbai's only serving encounter specialist and an able marksman, Vijay Salaskar was among the first ones to get a call after the mayhem at Leopold Café. Salaskar had reached his residence in Goregaon (in the western suburbs) before the shootout began and had relieved his driver for the day.

When the news of the attack poured in, Salaskar jumped into his vehicle and rushed towards South Mumbai. On the way, Salaskar got a call from his superiors informing him that a couple of suspects had been rounded up at the Colaba police and he should rush there.

Salaskar reached Colaba police station and questioned two foreign nationals. When he found that they were clean, he asked them to go and informed his boss and chief of the Mumbai crime branch, Rakesh Maria, about it. Maria had been asked by the commissioner of police to take charge of the main control room and handle the crisis from there.

Maria instructed Salaskar to rush to the police headquarters where all the crime branch officials had been asked to assemble so that they could chalk out a plan of action.

Salaskar left from Colaba along with a colleague. When he reached CST station he saw heavy police cover near Capitol cinema situated opposite the railway station. He asked a policeman about what was happening. The policeman informed him that two gunmen had broken into Cama Hospital.

Salaskar decided to rush towards Cama Hospital too, even though his colleague urged him to go to the crime branch. Salaskar also went beyond the call of duty and rushed towards the hospital.

When Karkare entered the Anjuman lane, Kamte had already reached there and had taken position behind a Qualis van belonging to an Assistant Commissioner of Police. Karkare also took position behind the Qualis as Salaskar joined them.

The trio was informed that Additional Commissioner of Police (Central Region) Sadanand Date and a few officers had also gone into the hospital.

Another officer who went beyond the call of his duty, Date along with a few officers from the Azad Maidan police station had managed to enter the hospital premises from its main entrance.

While they were waiting at the entrance and studying the situation they knew they did not have adequate manpower or firepower. They asked the control room to send additional forces while they blocked the exit to ensure that the gunmen did not escape.

A few moments later, a man came running down the stairs. He informed Date that the gunmen had gone to the terrace and there were at least 25 people who were hiding and could be taken hostage. Date knew that he could not risk the life of 25 people, so he decided to get up there regardless of the fact that his team didn't have enough weapons. There were seven officers including Date and they were armed with two service revolvers, a semi automatic machine gun, and Date's own revolver. With this he had to fight gunmen who were armed with sophisticated AK-47s and grenades.

Date and his team took the elevator and went till the fifth floor, because if the *fidayeens* were on the sixth floor they would be sitting ducks in the elevator.

Leading his team, Date took the stairs and reached the sixth floor. He asked his men to take positions and ensure that they were well covered. There was deathly silence on the veranda and visibility was zero because the lights had been switched off.

There was also a possibility that the *fidayeens* would have already changed their location or could have taken the 25 people hostage. To find out the exact location of the gunmen, Date picked up a stone and threw it towards the door of the terrace. Within a fraction of a second, a shower of bullets came through the door.

This trick not only helped Date assess the location of the *fidayeens*, but also helped save the lives of four people. The gunmen had found four people who were hiding in the terrace and had just then turned to shoot them. Their attention was diverted when Date threw the stone. The four hostages hid again.

The gunmen were now worried about the cops barging onto the terrace and took position with their guns pointing towards the entrance.

After a standoff for some time, Date and his team tried one more trick. They pressed the elevator button and sent it to the sixth floor. The moment the empty elevator reached the sixth floor, it was attacked with a hail of bullets and a grenade was lobbed towards it.

Such was the intensity of the gunfire that two officers were hit by bullets that had ricocheted after hitting the lift door. The grenade explosion seriously injured Date and other officers.

After the shooting stopped, Date instructed two of his officers to rush down and alert the control room. Date who was hurt quite seriously, decided to hold on and ensure that the gunmen did not escape till additional forces arrived.

The standoff between Date and the two gunmen lasted for almost 40 minutes. While the standoff continued – Karkare, Kamte and Salaskar were planning on how they could attack the gunmen. They decided that while Date engaged them on the sixth floor they would cover the main entrance.

The additional force with them was asked to cover the back door and other exits. While they were preparing to leave, a hand grenade exploded a few yards away from them. The *fidayeens* had noticed their movement and had hurled the grenade in their direction.

Kamte immediately opened fire from his AK-47. The

fidayeens were rattled by this, because this was the first time that they had been fired at by an AK-47. Kamte's shots were precise and the gunmen were flustered by this – they decided to flee.

The gunmen lobbed two grenades, one after the other, on the sixth floor. The explosion and shrapnel injured Date and he fell unconscious. Assuming that Date and his men had been killed and taking cover in the thick smoke caused by the explosion, the gunmen fled and walked down the stairs.

As they left the premises, one of the injured officers who had taken cover in the bushes saw them leave and informed the control room immediately. Another officer managed to rush to the place where Karkare and others were standing and informed them that Date had been injured and the gunmen had fled.

Within moments they heard gunshots from the direction of St. Xavier's College and Rang Bhavan.

After leaving the premises of Cama Hospital, the gunmen started walking in the direction of St. Xavier's College on Mahapalika Marg. They were stopped by a policeman who mistook them to be college students. The officer told them that there was a gunfight at Cama Hospital and they should not venture out. But, by the time the officer realised his mistake it was too late because a bullet had pierced his heart.

As they approached the lane of Rang Bhavan, they saw a

car with a red beacon coming out. It was the official car of the Health Secretary of the government of Maharashtra. The Secretary had asked his driver to get the car following the terror attacks.

The driver, Madhukar Phad, who resides in Rang Bhavan lane, was about to exit the lane, when the two gunmen stood in front of him. They planned to hijack the vehicle. Sensing danger, Phad reversed the vehicle and started going backwards. Ismail and Ajmal fired at the vehicle and severely injured Phad on his shoulder.

Phad immediately locked the doors from inside and reclined his seat and lay motionless. One of the bullets fired by the gunmen, had pierced the tyre, making the vehicle useless. Ismail and Ajmal decided to enter the lane.

Karkare and others who heard these gunshots, decided to rush in that direction. Since the Qualis van was the only available vehicle at that time, all of them got into it.

Salaskar, known to be a brilliant driver, took the driver's seat, while Kamte armed with his AK-47 sat in the front seat next to Salaskar. Karkare sat alone in the middle row and four constables including Salaskar's driver and Kamte's bodyguard sat behind.

As they turned left from the special branch office towards Rang Bhavan, Ismail and Ajmal who were standing at the entrance of the lane saw the vehicle and took cover.

Just as their van reached near an ATM centre of a bank opposite the Rang Bhavan entrance, the ever alert Kamte spotted Ajmal hiding behind the bushes. Kamte signaled Salaskar to slow down and fired from his AK-47. The very first shot hit Ajmal on his hand and his weapon fell. Salaskar stopped the vehicle and Kamte took position.

When Ajmal attempted to pick up his weapon, Kamte fired one more round, seriously injuring Ajmal's same hand. Salaskar fired from his 9mm revolver and hit Ismail on his leg.

In retaliation, Ismail who was lying down on the ground fired a volley of bullets towards the officer. Such was the salvo that before any of the officers could react they were all badly hit.

Karkare and Kamte died on the spot while Salaskar was severely injured. Even the four constables who were in the back seat were seriously injured.

Seizing the opportunity Ismail rushed towards the vehicle and removed Salaskar from the driver's seat and threw him on the ground. While Ajmal picked up his AK-47 and sat in the middle row after taking out Karkare's body from the van.

The duo hijacked the vehicle and fled leaving behind three brave officers who went beyond the call of their duty to protect the city. Ismail and Ajmal probably did not realise that their bullets had killed three of the best police officers ever seen by the Mumbai and Maharashtra police.

After hijacking the police van, the duo now were looking for a place where they could take a breather and call their handlers in Pakistan to find out what to do next. As they approached Metro Cinema junction, they fired indiscriminately at the media contingent and policemen who were standing there.

The media persons and police personnel were caught unawares because they thought it was only a police van. An officer of the crime branch standing there was hit by a bullet and died.

Even though Ismail and Ajmal had hijacked the police van, they did not realise that the bodies of the constables who were sitting in the backseat were still lying there. They realised this when a mobile phone belonging to one of the constables started ringing while they were driving towards Eros Cinema.

They thought that all four constables had died and Ajmal fired once again at the back seat. But as luck would have it, Salaskar's driver, Arun Jadhav, who was injured and lying below the bodies of the other constables was still alive.

Jadhav realised that he was in a situation where he could die any moment. "Even the slightest movement from me would have alerted them," Jadhav recalled. Jadhav hoped that the mobile phone didn't ring again. His eyes were locked on the wireless set which was lying beneath the middle row seat. He was hoping that the wireless set didn't crackle. Because that would also have again alerted the *fidayeens* and they would have either destroyed it or they would have got all the information relayed from the control room.

11
The Mumbai Siege Ends

After more than two days of pure terror, citizens were relieved by the sight of the last of the *fidayeens* being thrown out of the window on the ground floor of the Taj Mahal Hotel.

It was a moment with numerous definitions to it – a shocked and panicked nation heaved a sigh of relief when they saw this image live across all national and international news television channels. It was also a message to Islamic radicals to not mess with Indians any more. But most importantly, it signaled the end of a siege which had shattered and shocked the nation and the world alike. It was a sign of victory – the Indian security forces had finally triumphed in eliminating terror, after a 60-hour intense gun battle unlike anything history could have prepared them for.

The city hadn't slept for three nights and the sight of the dead *fidayeen* being thrown out had a calming effect on the citizens.

Within minutes, the chief of the National Security Guards (NSG) J K Dutta announced that the *fidayeens* had been eliminated and Taj had been taken. The NSG chief's announcement was welcomed by a loud cheer and rousing patriotic slogans by people gathered outside the hotel.

The bravery of the NSG commandos was applauded as they came out of the hotel. The snipers were showered with roses by the now pleased citizens.

Surrounded by the media and public, the otherwise invisible commandos enjoyed their well-deserved moments of national and international fame. "It was an easy operation, we took time because we weren't sure if the *fidayeens* had any hostages with them," said a commando as he walked out of the hotel.

Another commando said that he had always dreamt of visiting the heritage luxury hotel, but never thought that he would get a chance like this.

Hours after the horrendous Mumbai siege got over there began a battle within the country. Political parties indulged in the 'blame game' and politicians started targeting their political enemies rather than getting together and ensuring that the people of the country felt safe.

The first victim of this political feud was Union Home Minister Shivraj Patil. Already under a lot of fire after a series of bomb blasts across the country, the Mumbai attacks were the proverbial last nail in the coffin for Patil.

An impromptu peace march organised by netizens and

attended by millions of citizens saw the anger of the public out in the open. Everyone had realised that the real villains were the politicians. The cops, whom the citizens usually hated, had become their heroes. The citizens had seen the way the ill-equipped policemen had fought the *fidayeens*.

Looking at the sea of angry people and listening to their anti-politician sentiments, Maharashtra Chief Minister (CM) Vilasrao Deshmukh had to step down from his post. Deshmukh had come under a lot of criticism because he had taken his son, a film star, and a famous film director for what looked like a tour of the terror struck Taj.

The state's Deputy CM and Home Minister (HM) R R Patil too came under a lot of flak for the police's inability to prevent the attack despite there being enough intelligence inputs. But what cost Patil dearly was his poor knowledge of Hindi.

While addressing a media conference, Patil said in Hindi that small incidents like these terror attacks kept happening in a big city like Mumbai. What he probably meant was completely different, but this statement was beamed all across television channels over and over again.

An embarrassed and angry Patil called it quits.

The new CM Ashok Chavan and HM Jayant Patil immediately got into damage control mode and announced a series of policies and decisions to ensure that 26/11 would never be repeated.

Interestingly, a majority of the policies and decisions announced by the state government had already been approved a long time ago, but hadn't been worked upon. It indicates that had the politicians been proactive rather than reactive, 26/11 might never have happened.

12
Survivor Stories

He surivived two terror attacks.

A young British actor who played one of the London suicide bombers in a TV documentary faced a real life terror attack in the Mumbai massacre and was left for dead by gunmen before being detained as a suspect by the police.

Escaping death at the hands of real life *fidayeens*, Joey Jeetun, 31, who played suicide bomber Shehzad Tanweer in a British television documentary *7/7: Attack on London*, was in Leopold Café that night.

(1) Jeetun told the *London Times* how he survived the attack because the *fidayeens* assumed he was dead as he was covered in other people's blood.

"It sounded like they sprayed bullets at everyone and then looked to see who was alive and then started shooting them on the floor," he said.

"After about five minutes (the shooting) stopped and I opened my eyes. There were dead people next to me who had been shot in the head. I was scared, I was confused, I was distraught ... As an actor you can play a character, but this wasn't playing, it was real," he told a foreign news channel.

Jeetun from Bethnal Green, East London, said he owed his life to a stranger who jumped on him when the firing started at the Café.

In the chaos that followed, the Mumbai police mistook the actor for one of the *fidayeens* and was locked in a cell for 13 hours before they were convinced he was a genuine British tourist.

"I was held in a police cell for 13 hours with a group of Arab-looking men. They thought I was a suspect even though I told them I was a British tourist," he told another London newspaper.

Jeetun was born and raised in London and his mother is from the tropical island of Mauritius.

(2) Raj Kishore Partho cannot believe his luck. He has the distinction of surviving two terror attacks in Mumbai. Partho came to Mumbai 12 years ago. He had set up a coffee vending machine in the premises of the McDonald's outlet on the Mumbai Central railway station in 2002. On December 6, 2002, a bomb exploded in the outlet, Partho however escaped unhurt.

On November 26, Partho opened his coffee shop on CST platform at 9am. The day was just like any other day with thousands of commuters walking past his shop, some stopping over for a cup of coffee.

At around 9.40pm, with the day winding up, Partho was starting to wrap up his day. He had to count his earnings for the day, tally accounts and clear his register before closing his shop.

A regular customer came to the shop and Partho gave him a cup of coffee when all of a sudden a loud explosion shook the station. A burst of cracker-like sounds were heard and Partho saw people running for their lives. Before he could comprehend what was wrong, Partho saw a man running towards the exit his shirt was soaked in blood and was shouting. Partho realized that something was wrong.

Partho quickly glanced in the direction from where the sounds were coming, he saw two youngsters firing randomly at people. His first reaction was to lock the cash-box and run for life.

While running he saw injured people lying in pool of blood. People were screaming and running for life. A shocked Partho took cover near a bus stop across the road and waited for the situation to return to normal.

Since he had left his shop open, Partho returned after the situation became normal at around 2am. He locked his shop and went home. He returned to work next day on time but this time he was very scared. "I didn't feel anything during the bomb blast on Mumbai Central station in December 2002, because it all happened in a fraction of a second. This was horrifying because you could see death walking right in front of you," Partho recollected.

(3) Muneer Al Mahaj, an Iraqi citizen, was among the first batch of 93 guests to be rescued from the Trident on Friday morning. The hotel authorities had hired special luxury buses to take the rescued guests to another hotel.

He was instantly surrounded by media persons who wanted him to share his experience. Mahaj had come to Mumbai on a business trip with a friend. He was staying on the fourth floor of the hotel when the *fidayeens* stormed the place.

A scared and confused Mahaj locked himself in his room and switched on the television to find out what was happening. A few minutes later, the intercom rang, it was the hotel administration informing him that the hotel was under attack from armed gunmen and that he should stay inside his room till further instructions.

Mahaj followed the instructions and stayed indoors for almost 40-hours before he was rescued by a team of NSG commandos and hotel staff.

He had survived the 40-odd hour ordeal by eating only biscuits and drinking water.

On his way out, when Mahaj saw the mayhem caused by the *fidayeens* and the numerous dead bodies lying in the hotel premises, he considered himself lucky to have not run into a gunman.

A relieved Mahaj boarded the bus which would take him to a hospital for medical examination, but not before pledging to come back again to Mumbai.

(4) Deven was playing all by himself in the lobby outside Shamiana (a restaurant in the Taj Mahal Hotel), when suddenly he saw people screaming, shouting, and running. Ten-year-old Deven did not know what to do. He was too young to understand what was happening.

A hotel staff member who was meeting a couple of friends in the lobby also saw people running towards the main exit. Without hesitating, the staff member and his friends also ran towards the exit when they came face-to-face with the *fidayeens* who were still shooting.

They started running back towards the lobby, and saw Deven standing there, too stunned to move, was jostled away from his parents in the melee that followed. The staff member picked him up and ran towards a book shop. All four of them took refuge there trying their best to be out of the way of the gunmen.

After taking refuge, they switched off the lights in the shop and waited with bated breath. They heard muffled cries from inside the shop. They saw a woman crouched in the corner of the room, crying. Her husband had been shot in the lobby and he was dead. Her cries were drowned in the continuing storm of bullets and explosions that tore through the heritage structure.

Meanwhile, the staff member and his friends who had rescued Deven, tried to contact his parents who were dining in Shamiana. Thankfully, shaken up by the ordeal, Deven remembered his mother's mobile number. The hotel staff even sent a text message on the cell phone of his mother. But there was no way they could find out if she got the message.

With the entire ground floor plunged in darkness and no pause in gunfire, they decided to stay put. After almost three hours, the shots stopped and after some more time had passed, the boy, the three men and the woman, decided to take a chance and try to escape. The staff member decided to wait behind as he had to take care of the other guests.

They simply walked out of the store and through the darkened lobby, too scared to think about anything else, but if they would make it out alive or not.

All of them made it to safety. The second they stepped outside, they were pulled into safety by the police who arranged to take them home.

One of the rescued persons – a businessman, took Deven with him to his home on Peddar Road. On reaching home, he telephoned Deven's mother. It was a huge relief when Deven's mother answered the phone. She was extremely worried and anxious about Deven, but when she came to know that her son was safe and sound she heaved a sigh of relief.

The parents immediately rushed to the businessman's home and were reunited with their son almost ten hours after they were separated when the firing began.

(5) Shabana Shaikh, a resident of Akola district, Maharashtra, had come to Mumbai with her husband and son, for her husband's medical treatment. At around 9.30 pm on November 26, Shaikh and her husband Altaf and son Zubair, were waiting in CST railway station to go back home.

Shaikh was sitting on the platform with her husband and son. They had managed to get tickets for a train which was scheduled to leave at 11 pm. They sat quietly, tired after making rounds of several hospitals in the city, and then suddenly, they heard gunfire.

Instinctively, Shaikh covered her son and pinned him down to the ground. A bullet hit her hand and she fell unconscious. Her quick thinking had saved her son's life.

For the next few minutes Shaikh was on the floor,

injured and unconscious. She regained consciousness the next day in the hospital. When she enquired about her son and husband, her relative told her that her son was at home and unhurt, but did not give a satisfactory answer about Altaf.

Shaikh instantly knew something was terribly wrong. When she didn't let up asking about him, her relative told her that Altaf had been shot dead.

Shaikh could hardly help remembering that in the afternoon on that fateful day, the entire family had offered prayers at Haji Ali Dargah before going to CST.

(6) Viju Chauhan was in labour by the time she reached the maternity ward of the Cama and Albless Hospital at around 9 pm on November 26. She was a 27-year-old resident of the slums in Cuffe Parade, had no idea that she would always remember this day for several reasons.

Her labour pains probably started at the time when the ten *fidayeens* reached the shores of Mumbai at around 8.30 pm.

Chauhan was flagging down a taxi from near their house in Cuffe Parade, at around the same time when the *fidayeens* were getting into taxis from the Machchimar Colony only a few meters away.

Accompanied by her husband Raju and elder son, Chauhan reached Cama Hospital at around 9 pm.

Looking at her advanced stage of labour, the doctors rushed her directly to the labour room.

Raju proceeded to complete the registration. Just as the formalities were getting over, Chauhan was admitted to the pre- and post-natal wing on the third floor, and the sounds of gunfire were heard from CST station, a few meters away.

After several moments, the sounds of gunfire and explosions stopped. The puzzled Raju didn't know what was happening, but got worried when a hospital staff ran in, looking very scared. He told everybody that a security guard in the hospital had just been shot dead.

The hospital staff swung into action and herded all the relatives, including Raju, into the delivery room and shut the doors from inside. The metal beds were piled over each other and used to block and barricade the door.

After a while, they heard the *fidayeens* storming up the stairs. They shot at the door of the ward and some of the glass shattered. They banged the door with their guns and then they went on upstairs, recalls Raju.

There was a short burst of gunfire every two or three minutes. One of the hospital staffers informed the waiting relatives that the two gunmen looked like terrorists and asked everyone to be very quiet.

Chauhan was rushed into a small delivery room with a few doctors and nurses. Unable to gauge the seriousness outside because of the pain she was in, Chauhan thought she heard some firecrackers outside.

In the midst of all the noise and terror, the extremely brave doctors and nurses helped Chauhan deliver a baby girl. It was only after her little one was born, that Chauhan was told that the hospital was under siege.

Raju who had been confined in another room, had last seen his wife being rushed into the delivery room. A nervous and extremely anxious Raju wanted to know what was happening to his wife. However, it was only next morning that the authorities allowed people to move around.

Raju was delighted to learn that his wife and his little angel had survived the onslaught. An overwhelmed Raju wrote a letter to the hospital doctors, nurses and staff, expressing his gratitude to them. "I wrote to them in my mother tongue, Kannada, and thanked them for ensuring a safe delivery for my child, in such horrible circumstances," Raju said.

Raju hails from Karnataka in South India and works at the Sassoon Dock in Colaba. He and his wife have named their daughter Kranti, a symbol of hope to overcome the dark day on which she was born.

(7) In a stunning display of courage, a senior citizen who was inside the Cama and Albless Hospital fought the *fidayeens* when he came face-to-face with them.

Recollecting the incident while lying on a hospital bed, Harishchandra Shrivardhankar, a resident of Kalyan, said that he was trying to get inside one of the hospital rooms when the *fidayeens* came up from behind him.

Left with no choice, Shrivardhankar decided to fight the *fidayeens* rather than become an easy victim. On seeing him, the duo first attacked him with a knife and then hit him with the butt of an AK-47.

Just as they pointed the assault rifle towards Shrivardhankar to shoot, he leapt towards them, and hit one of them in the groin with his knee, and hit him again on the head with his carry bag.

The angry *fidayeens* slashed his neck and fired at him and ran up to the terrace. Two bullets hit Shrivardhankar in the back and he suffered two deep gashes on his neck. Due to the injuries and heavy loss of blood, he collapsed unconscious.

After the Cama Hospital encounter was over, police and rescue personnel rushed an unconscious Shrivardhankar to J J hospital and his family was informed.

(8) As a resident of Girgaum Chowpatty, Dinesh Gandhi is used to late night hustle-bustle at the main signal

of the chowpatty. Heavy presence of policemen at the signal is not a rare sight, but on the night of November 26, the police cover was abnormally heavy and there was an eerie silence as they moved around.

As Gandhi peered over his window and looked towards the signal, policemen were busy diverting traffic and restricting movement towards Nariman Point. They were also busy clearing up the streets and asking people and residents to stay indoors.

A diamond merchant, Gandhi was used to the late night nakabandis and checking by the police, but this was something else. The police had barricaded the entire road which came from Nariman Point and went towards Babulnath Temple. "It was unusual," recalls Gandhi.

The news of terror attacks had spread and everyone was glued to their television sets. But, the police were busy clearing the area as if they had some inkling that the *fidayeens* may come that way.

A little after midnight, Gandhi figured that the police activity around the signal had suddenly increased. There was tension in the air and all the policemen were armed and had taken strategic positions with their guns pointing in the direction of Marine Drive.

After a few moments, a car speeding from the direction of Nariman Point screeched to a halt a few meters away from the barricades. From a distance, policemen alerted the driver, shouted for the car to be stopped and asked him to come out. However, neither did the driver nor his companion come out.

As both the sides waited for the other to act, the car suddenly darted towards the barricades and just when it neared it swerved towards the right and tried to jump the road dividers. It however couldn't jump over and its right front tyre got stuck in the divider.

"After this, followed, a series of gunshots and lot of shouting and screaming," Gandhi said. However, within moments the gunshots died down and policemen and onlookers ran towards the car.

"It was only much later that we realised that one of the policemen Tukaram Omble had died after he valiantly captured one of the *fidayeens* alive, while the other was killed in the gun battle," Gandhi recalled.

(9) Kirloskar group chairman Vijay Kirloskar was at the Oberoi on the day terror struck Mumbai. The Bangalore-based industrialist, who had a miraculous escape, thanked his 50-year-long asthma problem for saving him from the 'worst time of his life.'

Kirloskar checked into the Trident on November 26 at around 10 am. He was attending a business meeting. Oblivious to what was coming his way, he came back to his room at 8.15 pm to rest for a while. "I was in room number 1460 on the fourth floor of the hotel along with my PRO John Samuel and

Pothiraj, my physiotherapist friend," recalls Kirloskar.

Ten minutes later Kirloskar and his friends heard something like firecrackers being set off outside their room. "It sounded like machine guns. I could sense something was wrong, but had no clue that it was terrorists," he said.

Kirloskar and his friends locked themselves up in the room and called up room service. "None of the lines were working. Even the TV set inside the room was disconnected. All we could hear was the noise of gunfire," he said.

At one point Kirloskar and his friends opened the door to see what was happening. "We saw a man near the lift who told us to lock ourselves up in the room and not come out," he said.

"At around 11.15 pm, we heard three big explosions, which I was told later were grenade blasts, outside my room. There was smoke and dust everywhere. The asthma made it tough for me to stay inside. Pothiraj and I put wet towels on the floor blocking the door but it was not helping much. The AC was pulling all the smoke inside," he said.

"I knew I had to make a choice fast. Either the *fidayeens* would get me or my asthma would, since my breathlessness was getting worse. We decided to take a chance. We took the map and headed towards the door. My eyesight is not good. Pothiraj helped me down the stairs and the three of us finally managed to escape through the emergency exit."

The businessman thanks his ailment for making him do the right thing. "It saved my life. God has given me the strength to cope with the situation and overcome the aftermath," Kirloskar said.

13
What Went Wrong: Intelligence Failures

December 12, 2006: The then Deputy Commissioner of Police (DCP) Dhananjay Kamlakar in-charge of the crime branch in Mumbai police had just received a vital Subsidiary Intelligence Bureau (SIB) input.

Kamlakar was startled. The tip-off was out of the ordinary: the Pakistani Navy was training Lashkar-e-Toiba *fidayeens*. It wasn't the crime branch's specialisation.

Crime branch officials had gunned down more than 600 gangsters in separate encounters in the past decade. Tracking *fidayeens* required different skills and a new breed of informers.

Kamlakar and his men were mostly dealing with underworld threats and gangland killings. After interrogating a few arrested militants the intelligence agencies learnt that a unit of the Inter Services Intelligence (ISI) in cooperation with a detachment from Pakistani navy, were imparting navigational training to LeT recruits.

There were others who were selected from Tanzeems (groups/organisations) like Hizbul Mujahideen and Jamait-e-Musalman. Indian intelligence agencies managed to elicit detailed plans about the training. They decided to share the information with police units across all states. The details of the plans were very alarming. For the first time, Pakistani naval personnel were imparting 12-18 month long navigation courses.

At that time, police officials could not gauge how naval training for terrorist trainees in Pakistan could affect the security of Mumbai. It made very little sense to officers trained to deal with organised crime syndicates and robbers in the city.

Kamlakar was worried about the security along the coastline of Mumbai. There were other details in the information he had received, such as the gruelling training taking place over three phases, which disturbed him.

In the first phase, the *fidayeens* were taught to swim. More worrisome was the fact that recruits were trained to handle large boats; plant mines in coastal zones and bombs under dams, bridges and ships in the second phase.

The final phase related to training in navigational techniques, rescue operations, surveillance methods, concealment of explosives, and underwater attacks on enemy targets and coastal vessels.

Intelligence reports also indicated that more than 500

fidayeens who have received navigational training in Pakistan are planning to infiltrate the country and island territories posing as fishermen. Many could use the porous Kori Creek zones to gain entry into India.

Similar warnings were sounded by the State Intelligence Department (SID) located at the Director General of Police headquarters in Colaba. SID was expected to liaise with other law-enforcement agencies across the state. The tip-off also warned about militant groups planning to attack important persons during the Republic Day function in 2007.

There was information about a possible kidnapping of a politician or an important person. The plan was to seek the release of Afzal Guru, the mastermind involved in the attack on the Parliament.

The various police departments were asked to keep a watch on the activities of gangs using the western coast and its corridors extending from the Gujarat coast to Mumbai. The results from such exercises turned out to be futile.

Nobody really knew what to look for and where. Police resorted to traditional Nakabandis and conducting searches in hotel rooms. The officials believed that these activities could help beef up security measures.

Kamlakar in an official letter (CW No 2575) instructed all 12 crime units comprising about 250 officers and constables to look out for information leading them to terror cells in Mumbai. They were even asked to beef up their intelligence gathering network with special emphasis on *fidayeens*.

The instructions didn't find favour with crime branch officials in Mumbai. There were not many *khabris* who could inform police about *fidayeen* networks. Even if they knew about the way *fidayeen* groups functioned, it wasn't easy to infiltrate their modules in the city.

In weeks, the information of a LeT attack in Mumbai was relegated to the background. Besides, routine crime in the city was keeping the policemen busy. Crime branch officials were still busy piecing together the information about a series of blasts that had ripped through suburban trains in Mumbai on July 11, 2006.

A steady flow of information continued to pour into the offices of all intelligence agencies in the country that LeT was planning to use the sea route to attack Indian cities when R&AW stumbled upon another interesting piece of information relating to the impending sea borne attack. It was critical.

Reports indicated that a senior LeT member Faisal Haroon was arrested when he was about to board a plane from Dhaka to Mauritius in 2006. The top leader was under the scanner of various intelligence agencies in the sub-continent for quite some time.

During questioning, Haroon told Bangladeshi authorities how LeT was using the sea route to smuggle RDX along the Gujarat coast to Mumbai and a few Southern states. The recipients were members of the homegrown militant outfits operating out of Hyderabad in Andhra Pradesh.

Bangladesh authorities deported Haroon to Pakistan soon after he was interrogated by local police. His release came as a shock to Indian authorities, who were waiting to pick him up at Mauritius. It was another big miss in a long list of misses.

Haroon's interrogation could have exposed Pakistan's plans to attack Mumbai. The identities of the *fidayeens* could have been known in advance and the Interpol could have been tipped-off in advance.

The newly formed ATS office was also inundated with reports warning about terror attacks. They were not taking chances. Senior officers like Joint Commissioner of Police and chief of the ATS K P Raghuvanshi and his deputy Param Bir Singh were busy analysing the threat perception.

ATS officials were not sure whether the threats were linked to Al Qaeda functionaries holed up in the Middle East, or was it local leadership. Questions were raised about links to the Gujarat carnage or violence in Kashmir. That the threat could be part of Al Qaeda's new global strategy was the theory doing the rounds in police circles in Mumbai.

Officials were left with little options but to beef up security along the coastal stretches at important installations like Bhabha Atomic Research Centre and other military targets within the reach of a possible Al Qaeda strike. Most of these tip-offs were fed by the central intelligence agencies.

The Indian Coast Guard had also intensified patrolling off the Maharashtra-Goa shores after receiving intelligence inputs that Al Qaeda leadership had sent a team to carry out attacks from the sea in early 2007.

A confidential report indicated that a group of militants frequented some islands along the west coast of the country. It was perceived that these islands were ideal spots for camouflaging sleepers or *fidayeens* in hiding before launching an attack.

The alarm bells were set off when Kasab, the only arrested *fidayeen* told investigators in Yemen that a member of their cadre had already surveyed one of the islands and efforts were made to win the confidence of local contacts.

The names of Yemeni militants Umar Barnuhriz alias Yasir Ahmed and Sultan Mubarak Binamardahalmeri alias Sultan Bin Mirda alias Abu-al-Hadrami figured prominently in the intelligence reports in the following weeks. Mohammed Kzekz had also visited some coastal tourist destinations in Maharashtra and the former Portuguese colony of Goa to carry out a thorough reconnaissance before a possible strike.

The police ran a background check on all visitors from countries affected by terror strikes. The Indian intelligence was led to believe that the Al Qaeda suspects had escaped the country after carrying out a recce of the region by early 2007.

The Indian Coast Guard had increased patrolling along the Goa-Karnataka-Kerala coast after they received information about the presence of Pakistani ISI operatives in the region. A fleet of three offshore patrol vessels were pressed into service to keep a lookout for suspect ships in the area. The results were not very satisfactory and there were not many interceptions.

There were also specific intelligence inputs about a consignment of counterfeit currency landings along the Bhatkal coast not far from Mangalore port which had been transported over land to some town in north Kerala. The Karnataka police had also proposed to set up dozens of police stations along the picturesque coastline to deter gangs of smugglers and LeT operatives working in tandem with ISI. These projects are yet to take off.

Even as various intelligence agencies were following the trail left behind by the terror suspects, Kerala Home Minister Kodiyeri Balakrishnan on July 24, 2007, told the Assembly that more than Rs 1000 crore had been routed into the state through hawala syndicates, many with links to anti-national forces.

Kerala constituted a four-member high level police team to deal with the hawala syndicates and coordinate with central intelligence agencies. A special team under Inspector General of Police Vincent M Paul was formed to tackle the hawala menace.

Intelligence reports indicated that the ISI had spread its tentacles down to the southern states and Kerala had become a hub of hawala transactions. It was reported that some of the money was wired to terror outfits across the country.

Bhatkal in Karnataka was under the surveillance of the Intelligence Bureau and other local agencies. The Coast Guard station close to Mangalore port was on the alert for any suspicious ships in the area. Kasargod, a nearby city, was also kept under observation by central intelligence field officers after there were reports that suspicious vessels were sighted in the littoral waters.

Pakistan-based fugitive gangster Dawood Ibrahim's key associate Aftab Bhatki was one of the main conduits for smuggling fake currencies into the country. He had acquired the nickname 'Bhatki' as he hailed from Bhatkal in South Karnataka. Intelligence reports indicated that Bhatki had been acting at the behest of the ISI and his mentor Dawood Ibrahim. He heads the syndicate from Dubai and Karachi.

Intelligence reports indicated that Bhatki and his associate Riyaz Bhatkal, another local gangster, was landing arms and huge consignments of counterfeit currencies in the area. The money was then transported by road to Kasargod.

Despite repeated intelligence inputs that Riyaz Bhatkal was

working for Laskhar-e-Toiba, very little efforts were made to track his movements or arrest him since 2003. In fact, not many officers in Mumbai police were aware that Riyaz Bhatkal was one of the wanted gangsters who were using the name RN. The gang was known as 'RN gang'.

Investigations into Riyaz Bhatkal's involvement as an LeT operative finally got a boost when crime branch sleuths under Joint Commissioner of Police Rakesh Maria learnt that Bhatkal was one of the founders of a terror outfit called Indian Mujahideen. In October 2008, Mumbai's crime branch team under Maria arrested eight suspects from Bhatkal. The police claimed they were members of the terror group, Indian Mujahideen. They were linked to Riyaz Bhatkal, who had masterminded a series of blasts across the country. However, crime branch sleuths were unable to elicit any information from the suspects that could have warned them about the impending terror attacks on Mumbai. This was despite the fact that some members of Indian Mujahideen were trained by Abu Hamza, who was entrusted with operations in India. Hamza was the common link between the Indian Mujahideen and LeT, both functioned under the umbrella of Al Qaeda.

After a series of bomb blasts across the country, Mumbai police and officers from central intelligence agencies started to believe that some members of the underworld could be working with the *jehadis*. This startling theory started gaining ground since it was noticed that *jehadis* do not use words like 'bastards', 'apes', and 'dogs' in their communications. Senior officers in Mumbai's anti-*fidayeen* squad raised questions about the role of some members of the underworld, particularly the 'D Company' in drafting sentences like 'eye for eye' prior to the Ahmedabad blast on September 13, 2008. The Al Qaeda manual clearly forbids the use of unparliamentary words while sending mails.

The Indian Mujahideen, which claimed responsibility for some blasts across the country, first made its appearance after the judgement was delivered by an upper court in 2007 about the Mumbai 1993 blasts case. The judge had delivered severe sentences. Fugitive gangster Dawood Ibrahim is one of the prime accused in the case.

Intelligence reports indicated that the funds for Indian Mujahideen were routed through Abdul Bari, a former resident from Hyderabad and now operating from the Gulf countries. Aeronautical engineer C A M Basheer from Kerala was also on the radar of the investigating agencies, but the trail had gone cold in the past few years. The killing of four Kerala youths in the northern state of Jammu and Kashmir had raised doubts that Basheer could have financed a few members of his cadre to undergo training in Pakistan. Investigations hinted that the slain Keralite youths were headed for camps in Pakistan.

Everything seemed normal on the surface. What officials failed to understand that deep down Pakistani ISI was creating a strong base to launch a sea-borne attack along the Western shores of the country.

Anti Terrorism officials launched another major combing

operation for LeT operatives after receiving vital tip-off on February 5, 2007. A high-level meeting between all top officials was held and senior inspectors attached to police stations near the sea were informed about the threat.

The two LeT men were identified as Abu Aquma and Abdulla. They were members of a squad trained by Abu Hamza, the man entrusted with leading operations in India.

ATS officials said that security along Mumbai's coastline would be strengthened. But there was nothing very specific or any leads to follow leading to the suspects.

A week later there was another intelligence report that the *fidayeens* could hijack a light aircraft or helicopter to carry out strikes in Mumbai. Security around Chhatrapati Shivaji International Airport was beefed up following the threat. The nuclear project at Bhabha Atomic Research Centre at Trombay was brought under heavy security cover. Defence establishments in and around Mumbai were put on high alert.

Bangladesh-based Harkat Ul Jihadi Islami (HuJI) also came under the scanner of the Indian agencies. It is being suspected that Pakistani ISI has been outsourcing terrorism through them. The outfit could have been roped in to provide logistic support in case of a planned attack on India.

In September 2008, field intelligence units of the Customs and Intelligence Bureau were receiving regular inputs about Pakistani fishermen slipping into Indian waters. Local *kharwas* or fishermen in Porbandar and Veraval in North Gujarat were talking about a group of trained commandos planning to come through the sea.

Some of the *Machis* in the area, who were Muslim fishermen, had also heard about Pakistani commandos attacking a hotel in Mumbai. The field intelligence units picked up these little bits of information and the fact that the Pakistan navy was training LeT men to attack targets in Mumbai.

The entire coastal stretch extending from Sir Creek to Okha is considered to be a strong base from Intelligence Bureau informers. They keep a lookout for any suspicious movement, particularly Pakistani fishermen, in the littoral waters. So strong is the network that every hamlet has over six informers on the payroll. The Gujarat coast has been notorious since the 1960s (1) Haroon Talab: A fisherman by profession, Haroon is considered to be the pioneer of smuggling in India. He started with smuggling gold in the 1960s and was active along the Kutch coast. (2) Ratilal Navik: An understudy of Talab, Navik took smuggling activities further and settled near the Surat coast. (3) Lalu Jogi: He also was a fisherman who later became a smuggler. Apart from smuggling gold, he ventured in smuggling electronic goods as well. He worked near the Daman coast. (4) Bana Khalap: Again a fisherman-turned-smuggler, was active at the Daman coast in the 1970s. (5) Sukur Narian Bhakia: He was among the last of the fisherman-turned smugglers, before the Indian government clamped down heavily on smuggling activities.

He too worked near the Daman coast.

Members of 'Operation Swan', a joint patrolling operation by the Customs, Navy, Coast Guard and local police, were aware of a similar plan about *fidayeens* trying to enter Indian waters, but the information was vague. It made little sense as the tip-off did not specify important details like place and time of attack. Other details like the kind of boat and crew would have helped.

The coastal patrols were put on high alert. The Pakistani navy had impounded 481 Indian fishing vessels for venturing into their waters. There was information that these boats could be used for *fidayeen* activities in India. While the various intelligence gathering agencies were busy assessing and piecing together bits of information, fishermen in Mumbai had heard about RDX being smuggled along the western seafront towards the commercial capital in August 2008. Again the tip-off was very vague and there weren't enough details to link the smuggled explosives to the perceived threats. The situation was grave, but the police could not come out in the open with these facts as it is difficult to fight a faceless enemy.

Fishermen along the Maharashtra coast were also gathering information that Pakistani *fidayeens* were waiting for the monsoons to get over so that they could set sail in calm seas. Again the report made very little sense to the various intelligence agencies and nobody was ready to believe that attacker would sail for four to five days to attack Mumbai.

'If the sea is bad for us, then it is bad for our enemies too,' remarked a senior Coast Guard officer.

Damodar Tandel, president of a fishermen' association met Maharashtra Deputy Chief Minister R R Patil in August 2008 and informed him about a possible attack from the sea. He also pointed how some government officers were involved in issuing fake licences to fishermen from Gujarat without proper verification of documents. Patil had assured Tandel that the matter would be looked into after the meeting. (The information could not be assessed for action).

In another major embarrassment, when the *fidayeens* set sail onboard the MV Kuber on November 23, they sailed right under the nose of a high profile naval exercise which was ongoing at that time in the seas off the coast of Gujarat.

The fishing trawler which was was ferrying 10 trained Pakistani *fidayeens* with a huge consignment of arms and ammunition for attacking Mumbai, slipped past a major naval exercise code named 'Defence of Gujarat'.

Dozens of naval, coast guard ship and fixed wing aircrafts had taken part in the operations. Even port workers and gram panchayat officials were included in the exercise, which started on November 17, 2008 and continued for more than a week.

The task was to track all vessels plying in the area and check their identities. In fact, it was a mock drill to track down Al Qaeda and Pakistani ships in the area. Threats to offshore oil platforms were part of the naval exercise. It was exactly during this period that *Kuber* cruised around the naval ships and headed for Mumbai, pointing to major security lapses on the part of various agencies.

It is not that the unfriendly crew of Kuber had not seen or expected? naval ships en route Mumbai. They used secret codes such as '*yaar logon ka group*' which meant a fleet of naval vessels. Civilian boats were referred as 'bhai log' and the voyage was called 'baraf' or ice.

Rules under the International Ships Port Security Code were also violated. Special security checks have been made mandatory by the International Maritime Organisation in the aftermath of 9/11 attacks in United States of America. In fact, it was difficult for port authorities and the Coast Guards to check the movements of about 80,000 fishing vessels, with around 44,000 registered in Gujarat alone. There is no system in place whereby an unfriendly vessel could be singled out and checked from a fleet fishing in the area.

The various security agencies were aware of intelligence reports that more than 440 Indian fishing boats were impounded by the Pakistani navy. These vessels could be used by terror outfits to infiltrate Indian waters after the monsoon, when the sea is calmer.

Even as the information was building up, the Research & Analysis Wing (R&AW) centre at Bhuj intercepted another important conversation on November 18, 2008. LeT key operative Muzammil alias Abu Yusuf was heard informing one of his associates in India that the cargo was on its way. The conversation was in Punjabi. R&AW operatives had heard about the training camps in Muzaffarabad in Pakistan Occupied Kashmir (POK). It was not difficult to infer that the deadly cargo could be trained fighters. Telephonic intercepts also indicated Muzammil requesting Bangladesh-base militant group Harkat Ul Jehad Islami leader Yahya to arrange for 35 SIM cards.

LeT operatives arranged for 32 SIM cards from Kolkata. Three were procured from New Delhi. Some of these cards were intended to be used during the planned terror attacks in Mumbai. These cards were to facilitate talks between the *fidayeens* and their handlers in Pakistan. The consignment of cards was smuggled through a contact in Pakistan Occupied Kashmir and the details of their movement was available to the intelligence agencies. Incidentally, the militant group took precautions not to activate the cards until the *fidayeens* had reached Mumbai. The information about the SIM cards was a very important lead available with the central intelligence agencies, but it required coordination between many police teams. Reports indicate that the cards were activated minutes before the 10 *fidayeens* landed in Mumbai, leaving very little time for the central intelligence agency and the police to close in on the LeT operatives. The agency could not link the SIM cards to impending attacks on Mumbai.

American Central Intelligence Agency's (CIA) station chief in New Delhi had also tipped off intelligence officials about a possible attack. CIA's independent network in Pakistan had warned about a group of trained fighters and it was obvious that they were being specially prepared for a mission. There were reasons to believe that the information was authentic.

Amidst the flurry of telephonic interceptions, R&AW's moles in Pakistan had been feeding their handlers in India about LeT training camps in POK. There were reports of a group of 32 men being trained in Muzaffarabad. They were trying to connect whether it was the same team which was intended to be sent to Mumbai.

R&AW's information centre had also picked up a conversation that some luxury hotels in Mumbai could be on the hitlist. This vital information was passed on to the Directorate of Intelligence Bureau (DIB). On November 19, 2008, R&AW passed on the information to National Security Council (NSC) and the National Security Adviser, both nodal agencies for assessing security information.

It was routine practice that the National Security Adviser forwards the information to the Joint Secretary In-charge of Internal Security. The information is then passed to the Chief Secretaries of the concerned states. The message was faxed with reference number 23-4405 to the Maharashtra government on November 19, 2008.

R&AW had also informed the Joint Intelligence Committee, who in turn passed on the information to state Subsidiary Intelligence Bureau (SIB). It is the SIB's job to pass on the information to the Commissioner of Police and Director General of Police in various states.

R&AW and SIB had almost similar standard operational procedures and almost the same kind of training for their officers. The equipment they used was also similar. But, the local police were a different lot. They did not have proper training for dissemination of such sensitive information and with regard to such terrorist-related activities, were not able to think and act fast.

There was more than one agency working on all the tip-offs received about a possible attack on Mumbai. However, ensuring that the information made its way past multiple agencies and officers was not easy. Therefore, no single agency could take charge of the situation. Intelligence driven action could not be carried out.

The Maharashtra government had prior information that *fidayeens* were planning a major strike in Mumbai. The cumbersome bureaucracy was unable to pass on the information in time to prevent the attack. This is mainly because of lack of coordination between the state and central intelligence agencies.

On November 27, 2008, the day after the attack, Deputy Chief Minister R R Patil told the press that the state government had received information about a LeT attack. The information lacked vital details to be assessed for action, he said.

WHAT WENT WRONG?

In November 2007, exactly a year before the attacks, the Intelligence Bureau (IB) had sent an alert to the

Maharashtra police that highly reliable intelligence inputs indicated that the LeT was planning a massive terrorist operation in India and the operation might involve *fidayeen* attacks, one-to-one firing and the use of grenades. It might also involve hostage-like situations, according to the input.

The IB as well as the Maharashtra police failed to take any action on this vital information.

In September 2008, when the Marriot Hotel in Islamabad was bombed, the IB once again alerted the Maharashtra police. This time it was more specific. The alert clearly stated that the LeT was planning a terror attack in Mumbai. The input even identified places like the Taj Mahal Hotel, Taj Land's End Hotel and the JW Marriot in Juhu as possible targets.

14
Did The *Fidayeens* Botch Up The Actual Plan?

Hours after the terror attacks in Mumbai started, the then Deputy Chief Minister R R Patil said that the *fidayeens* had enough ammunition to kill as many as 5000 people. Which means that the 26/11 Mumbai terror attacks could have been much worse. Experts who are involved in the clinical post mortem of the terror attacks feel that the *fidayeens* did not successfully execute their plan.

There was no doubt that they managed to completely shake and shock Mumbai, but those who studied the situation feel that apart from the attack on Nariman House, where the targets were clearly Israeli nationals, the *fidayeens* bungled the actual plan.

Consider the following lapses by the ten *fidayeens*:

Their handlers had asked them to sink the *MV Kuber* after they got on to the dinghy, the *fidayeens* didn't do that. Had they done it, the Indian investigators would have not found the crucial evidence onboard the *Kuber* which linked the *fidayeens* to Pakistan. Investigators would have never known how the *fidayeens* had entered the city.

They also had clear instructions to dispose the satellite phone once they reached Mumbai. This too did not happen. While talking to his handlers on the mobile phone from inside the Taj, a *fidayeen* said that they were nervous when an Indian patrol vessel came close to them when they were near Mumbai. They forgot to destroy the satellite phone. The recovery of the satellite phone was the most important evidence for investigators as it not only helped link the *fidayeens* to Pakistan. It was a link which even Pakistan could not deny.

The lone arrested *fidayeen*, Mohammed Ajmal Amir, during his interrogation revealed that their instruction from their bosses was clear – kill as many people as possible, then take as many hostages as the situation allows and head to a vantage point. After that, they were to prolong the gun battle for as long as they could.

However, they failed in this operation as well. Considering the number of people present in the two five-star hotels and the CST railway station, the *fidayeens* weren't able to take many hostages.

One of the biggest setbacks for the *fidayeens* and the terror group in Pakistan was the fact that Ajmal was captured alive. Being a *fidayeen* squad none of them were expected to be alive. But, thanks to Assistant Sub-Inspector Tukaram Omble of the DB Marg police station, a *fidayeen* was caught alive for the first time ever.

Ajmal is living proof of the involvement of Pakistan-based terror groups in the Mumbai attacks. Indian as well as foreign investigators have scientifically and painstakingly established that Ajmal belongs to Pakistan.

The experts also feel that the *fidayeens* did not have a Plan B. Neither were the *fidayeens* prepared nor trained to handle the quick retaliation from the ground level police force. During his interrogation, Ajmal said that their trainers in Pakistan had told them that there would be no retaliation from the ground level police force and they could just go on firing and take people hostage. But when the police retaliated within minutes both Ajmal and his partner Ismail did not know what to do and had to change their plans last minute.

Experts also felt that the *fidayeens* were not well versed with the topography of the hotels and the CST station.

Based on all these inferences, investigators feel that even though the *fidayeens* managed to create panic and horror and garner worldwide attention, had they been able to successfully implement the actual plan it would have been of humongous proportions.

15
The Plan And Strategies Made By Terror Outfits To Attack Mumbai

The seaborne attack on Mumbai was planned by Pakistani Inter Services Intelligence in early 2005. Intelligence reports available with the Mumbai police hinted that about 500 volunteers were being trained by the Pakistani Navy as marine commandos.

Based on the intelligence reports, the Mumbai police did have an idea that Pakistan-based outfits were planning an attack on Mumbai. But priorities and objectives of the department were different at that time. They could have refined the intelligence report and beefed up security along the coastline.

The 500 volunteers were selected for Daura-e-Khas, graduation from the Lashkar-e-Toiba terror schools. It was a kind of advanced training generally imparted to military personnel to whip them into shape.

Even some of the *fidayeens* involved in the blast in a train near Mulund railway station on May 13, 2003, had confessed that they had attended LeT training camps in Pakistan. The vital interrogation reports were buried under files and there was no synergy between the crime branch sleuths and officers from the central intelligence agencies.

Interrogation reports indicated that commandos were trained by the ISI and its affiliates like LeT and Jaish-e-Mohammed to destabilise India by systematic attacks. The plan was to spread terror and instill fear in the minds of Mumbaikars.

Fidayeens arrested by Indian security agencies told interrogators that it was not uncommon among operatives to switch from LeT to Jaish-e-Mohammed for ideological reasons. The Jamaat-ud-Dawa (JUD) also had an active role to play in the attacks on Mumbai. Pakistan pretended to launch a clamp down on JUD after the UN Security Council declared the organisation as a front for LeT, and Jamaat chief Hafiz Mohammed Saeed was placed under house arrest. The ban and the arrest did not work.

THE ORIGIN OF LeT

The Lashkar-e-Toiba (LeT) or the army of the pure, dates back to 1989 when it was founded by Hafiz Mohammed Saeed, a former teacher of Islamic studies at Lahore University. The philosophy is based on Wahhabism, the austere brand of Islam preached in Saudi Arabia.

In the past two years, LeT chief Zaki-ur-Rehman Lakhvi alias Chacha had handpicked 32 candidates for Mumbai attacks. Mohammed Ajmal Kasab was one of them. Lakhvi was assisted by Yusuf Muzzamil also known as Abu Ghure or Yusuf in the inner circles of the militant group. Lakhvi and Muzzamil were assigned the task of ensuring that the trainees could think and act fast. The strike team was taught to function in groups of two and four. They underwent special training at camps at Muridike, Manshera, and Muzzafarabad in Pakistan. These camps were called 'points'.

Standing tall at 6 feet 3 inches, Muzzamil was in-charge of attacks in Phulwama, Anantnag, Doda, and Kishwar districts on the Indian side of Kashmir. He was also entrusted with the additional responsibility of planning attacks on other parts of the country.

After receiving advanced training near Um-al-Qura and Mangla Dam, the camp was shifted to an isolated place near Karachi. The group was trained in marine commando tactics by retired Pakistani special forces officers.

The group was later trained by Abu Hamza and Kaahfa, both senior functionaries of LeT. This duo was the 'handler' the *fidayeens* spoke to during the Mumbai attacks. Zarrar Shah was assigned the task of liaising with the ISI for instructions and execution of the plan.

The volunteers were also given AK-56 assault rifles, which could fire in bursts of 600 rounds per minute. The Chinese-made weapons were far too superior compared to the 220-odd AK-47 rifles in the Mumbai police's arsenal.

Despite all the tip-offs, the seaborne attack had all the elements of surprise. ISI and LeT were aware that the Indian marine police were not trained to intercept a ship. Besides, the marine police were not armed with automatic weapons.

The port authority rarely scanned the seas for unfriendly vessels and rarely did officials board a suspect ship for inspection. There was no force ready to prevent an unfriendly ship from entering city waters.

The second phase of the plan was to launch several attacks at the same time. The *fidayeens* were told that the Mumbai police were not trained to handle these new tactics. In fact, it was a clear shift from the 'traditional' attack on a single area such as while fighting security forces in J&K. A shift from vehicle-borne to seaborne attacks; and the *fidayeens* acting in small groups of two and four, added to the woes of the Mumbai police, who had specialised in dealing with the underworld who had a different modus operandi.

The *fidayeens* were told by their handlers that the Mumbai police would panic on seeing a large number of casualties within the first few minutes of the attack. It would be a free run for the terrorists after that. The Pakistani trainers were almost right in their assumption, but the local police converged to throw a thin ring around the attackers.

The strike team that had set sail from Karachi in a small boat at around 8 am on November 22, 2008, after sailing for about 40 minutes the fidayeens were transferred to a larger boat Al Husenni. Already, there were seven LeT functionaries on board Husenni.

On the following day an Indian-registered trawler M V Kuber came along side Husseni around 3 pm. Four of the Indian crew members were asked to board the *Husseni* immediately. They were later killed and their bodies dumped into the seas.

Amar Singh Tandel, skipper of Kuber, was allowed to steer the vessel on its 550 nautical miles journey to Mumbai.

On board Kuber the 10 fidayeens were handed over haversacks containing AK-56 assault rifles, live rounds, Pakistani-made Diamond Nedi 9 mm calibre pistols, Austrian Ages hand grenades. There were many grenades manufactured by Pakistani at their ordinance factory near Rawalpindi and heaps of dry fruits to subsidise regular food. They were also given packets containing improvised explosive devices.

The fidayeens maintained watch duties in shifts keeping an eye for Coast Guard patrol boats. Kuber sailed close to Mumbai around 4 pm on November 26, 2008.

The plan was to strike under cover of darkness. The last leg of the cruise took them to Badhwar Park on Cuffe Parade at around 8.30 pm, almost four hours after *Kuber* came close to Mumbai harbour.

The multiple and simultaneous attacks had taken the Mumbai police by surprise. With the turmoil in Afghanistan and Pakistan, Mumbai could be in for many more serious shocks. The National Investigation Agency could be an answer to deal with attacks from radical Islamic groups.

The Face of Terror

The Taj: A room on the sixth floor after the carnage.

The Taj: The spectacular corridor on the sixth floor was reduced to ashes during the attack.

The Taj: The Harbour Bar witnessed some of the fiercest gun battles.

The Taj: The Harbour Bar lies in ruins while investigators gather evidence.

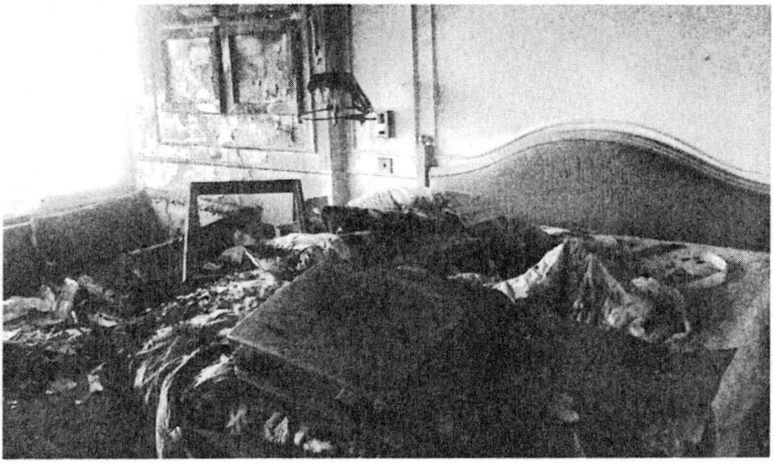

The Taj: One of the charred rooms on the sixth floor.

The Taj: The attack began at the poolside.

The Taj: media persons camped outside the Taj, in the line of fire.

The Taj: Commandos of the Mumbai Crime Branch take their positions as gunfire rings out.

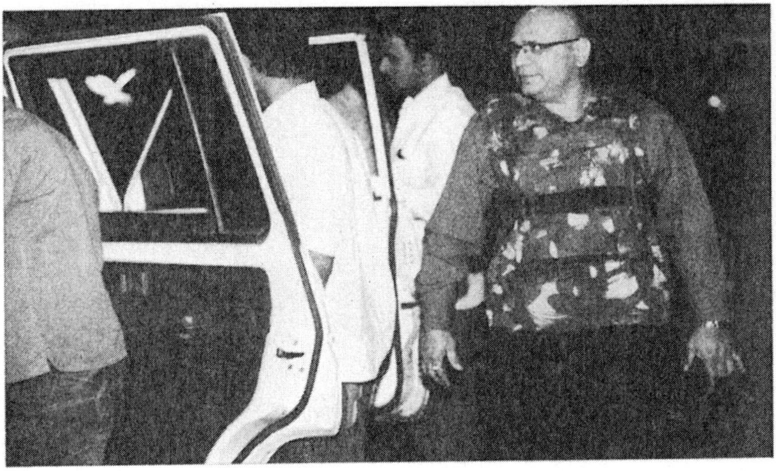

The Taj: An officer from Indian Army readies to battle the *fidayeens* on 26/11/2008.

The Taj: Despite the long-drawn out fight, the city's defenders stayed alert.

The Taj: An elderly person being carried out of harm's way by the police.

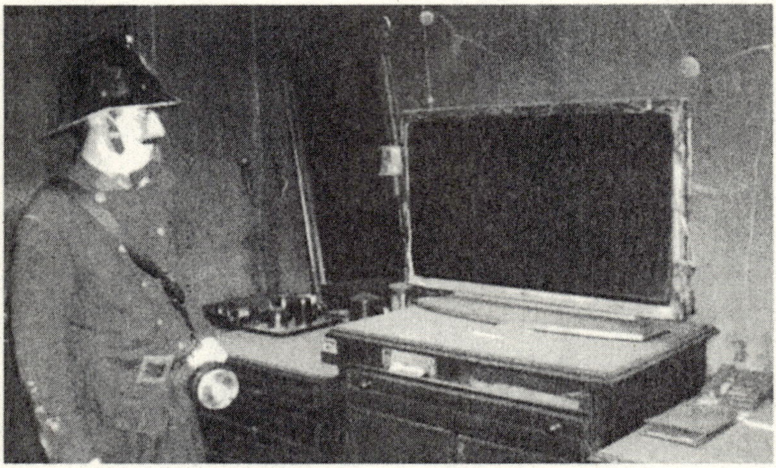

The Taj: A fireman inspecting the damage in one of the luxurious rooms.

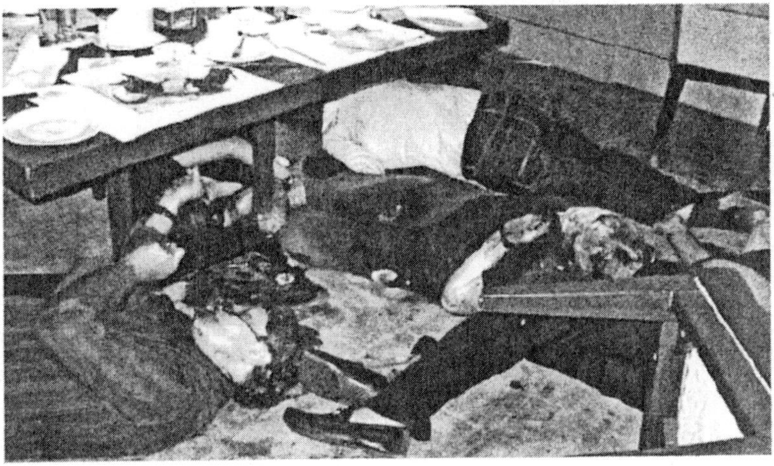

The Oberoi/Trident: Tiffin restaurant where several people became victims of terror.

Nariman House: A room in the little known home that witnessed the terror attack.

Nariman House: The bullet riddled walls bear testimony to the deadly terror attacks.

Nariman House: Rabbi Gavriel Holtzberg, his wife Rivika Holtzberg who were killed in the terror attacks at Nariman house.

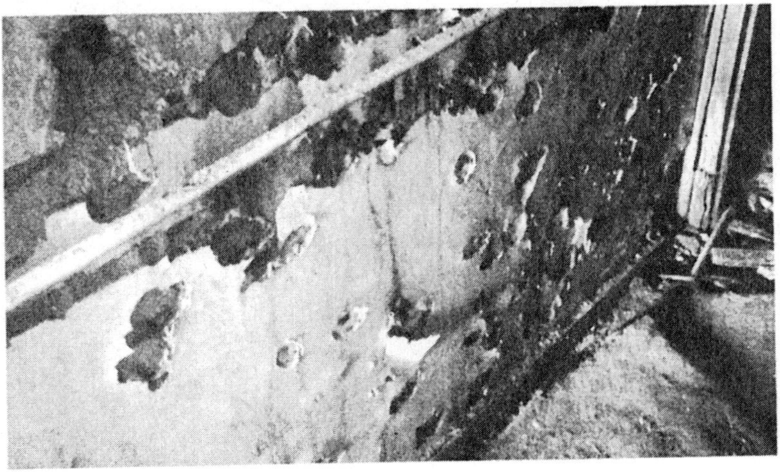

Nariman House: Bullets fired from AK-47 leave behind a gruesome reminder.

Nariman House: One of the rooms on the fourth floor that the *fidayeens* took over.

The bloodbath at CST station left many dead.

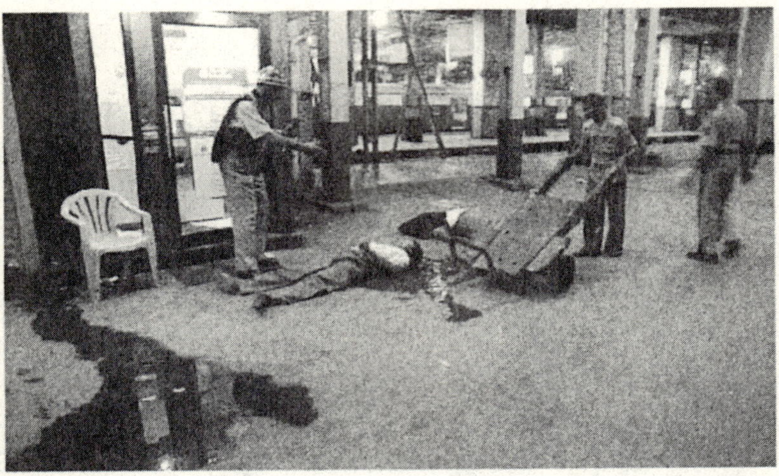

The attack on CST Station could have been worse.

CST Station: Home Minister P. Chidambaram reviewing the situation with senior officials on 6th December 2008.

CST Station: Police inspector Shashant Shinde was shot dead by the terrorists.

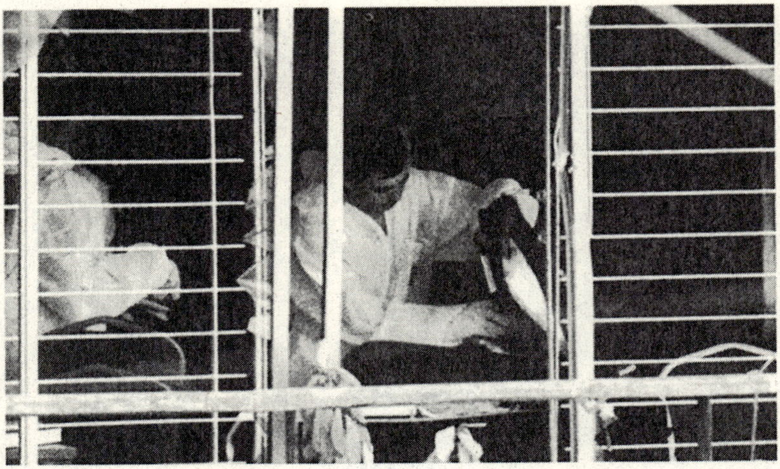

FBI officials collecting forensic samples to bottle the evidence against Pakistan.

A special team of FBI officials offered their help to India.

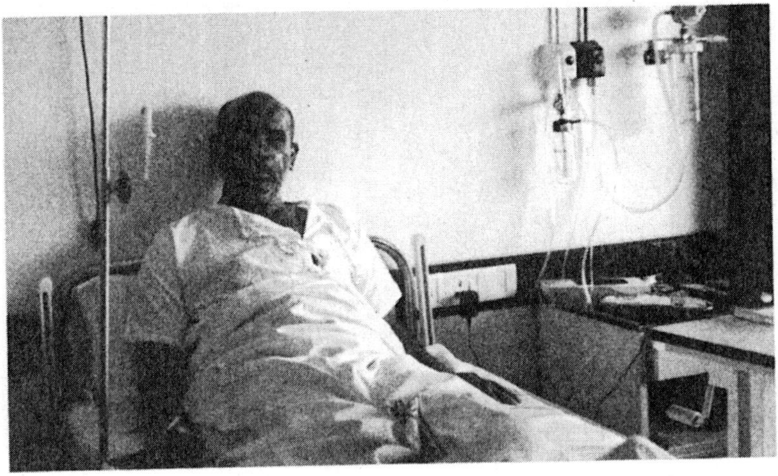

Deepak Dhole, inspector, suffered burn injuries while fighting *fidayeens* at the Taj.

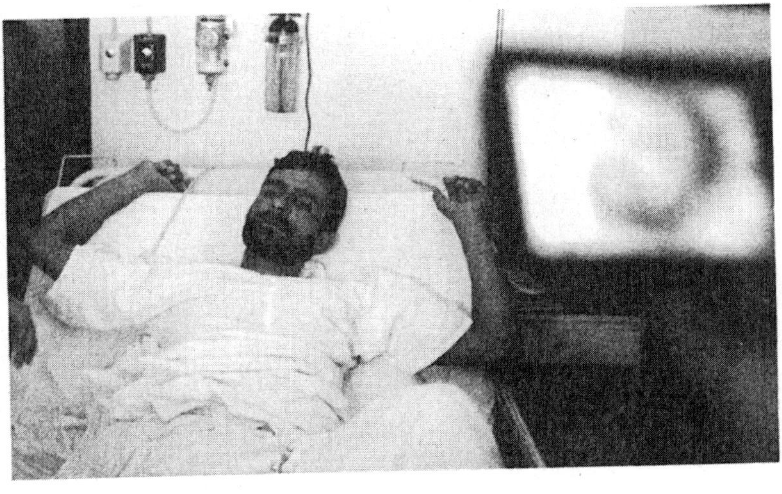

Sunil Yadav, a National Security Guard (NSG), was injured at Taj while rescuing guests.

MV Kuber: The fishing trawler in which the *fidayeens* came to Mumbai.

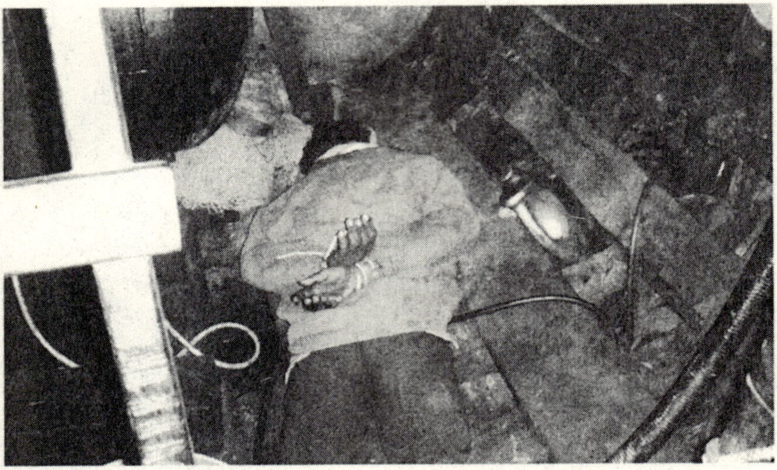

Captain of the trawler MV Kuber, Amar Singh Tandel, was murdered and his body was dumped in the engine room.

MV Kuber: Police check for evidence of the *fidayeens* handlers.

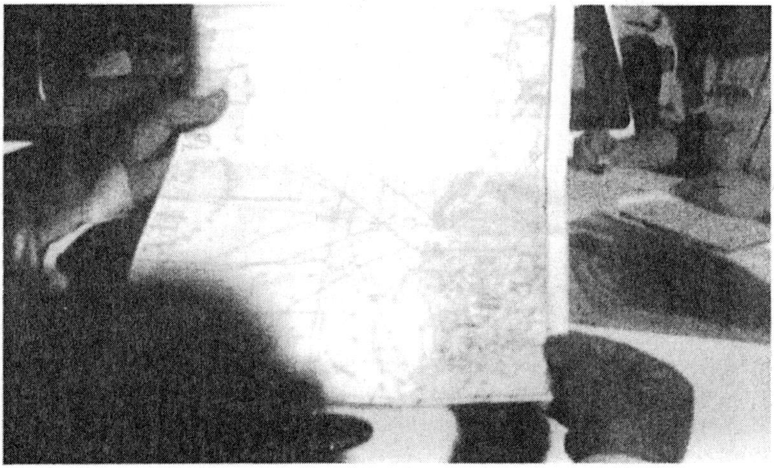

A map recovered from the trawler MV Kuber shows the route from Karachi to Mumbai.

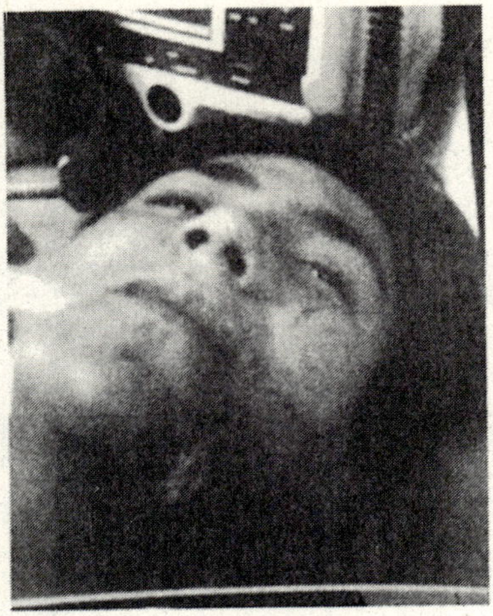

The lone arrested *fidayeen*—Mohammad Ajmal Amir Kasab at Nair Hospital.

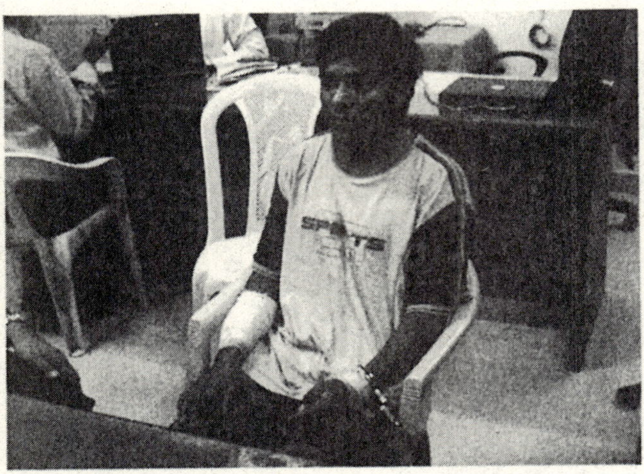

Kasab in police custody.

16
Precautions

By GVK Unnithan

India has over 7600 kilometers of coastline and an Exclusive Economic Zone (EEZ) of approximately 2 million sq km. The area around the exploratory fields and off-shore installations admeasuring 20,000 sq km is out-of-bounds for ordinary vessels. These areas are well defined, isolated on the charts, marked with buoys, physically patrolled by boats and subjected to electronic surveillance. There is always a flurry of activity around the oil fields, night and day.

Various types of vessels and other specialised crafts including helicopters keep flying in and out of this region round the clock. A centralised security agency under the Indian Navy, and the Offshore Defense Advisory Group (ODAG) funded by the petroleum ministry and oil majors, keep surveillance of the restricted areas around the exploratory and production sites. This agency deals with response measures in case of maritime disasters, namely fire, collision, grounding, oil spill etc, and undertake major salvage operations. The ODAG depends on hired vessels for patrolling. As of January 2009, the Government has decided to empower this Group with more responsibilities and to give it more assets.

There are several problems with coastal patrolling as there are about 3000 fishing vessels of various types, sizes and shapes in the EEZ at any given time. Though there are certain set patterns and schedules observed by these off-shore and deep sea fishing crafts, it may not be an easy task to track every vessel plying in the area. These boats and crews have their own identity documents that are liable for production for verification to security forces. However, checking the documents of the crew members by going along side poses several problems. In fact, it is difficult to bring the fishing boats close to the inspecting vessel. The trawling lines and nets cause serious threats to the inspecting ships. Also, it is dangerous to sail close to them and check their movements.

Identification from a distance is not a practical solution either. As in the case of the Mumbai attacks where the LeT operatives commandeered a trawler registered in Gujarat. This is not an isolated case. There are scores of fishing boats registered in other states and ports. There are other types of traditionally built heavy wooden sailing crafts, Mechanised Sailing Vessels (MSV) known by different names, such as *dhows*, *bagalas*, *kotias* and *thonis*. They generally sail between the Arabian and African coasts and are operated by local seamen from Gujarat. Sailors from Kutch in Gujarat, Ratnagiri in Maharashtra, and

Tuticorin in Tamil Nadu, are nominally under the control of the Director General Shipping (Sails). The travel documents of these country crafts are out dated and obscure. Often security concerns surrounding these sailors are overlooked. In most cases, they manage to operate without valid travel documents or passports.

Multiple agencies manage the onion-like multiple layers of coastal security – the state police guard the territorial waters or the distance between the lowest low water mark out to 12 nautical miles; policing the 12 to 200 nautical miles, i.e. the Exclusive Economic Zone, is the responsibility of the Coast Guard. Beyond that, the writ of the Navy runs. Gujarat and Maharashtra coasts are intensively patrolled by the combined forces of the Customs, Marine Police and Coast Guard, while the Southern Tamil Nadu coast is patrolled by the Police, Coast Guard and Navy. While there are no restrictions on boarding a foreign vessel in the territorial waters, that of boarding them for inspection within our EEZ is to be exercised with caution.

Unlike land patrols, those at sea are highly monotonous. Crew fatigue is considerable. Inspection of individual fishing boats is highly time consuming and virtually impossible. This could be obviated to certain extent by fixing identifying equipments on board, but crew identification would remain a distant reality. Intelligence reports have indicated that the Pakistani Navy is training LeT and Jaish-e-Mohammed *fidayeens*. Recruits are being taught to destroy ships at harbour and marine infrastructural facilities. How does one guard against such terror attacks?

There has to be political will and greater defense management. Only the strictest vigil will counter future *fidayeen* exploits.

One of the most important measures announced by the government is the formation of a Coastal Command headed by a naval Vice Admiral and the responsibility of coastal patrolling and its defense has been transferred to the Coast Guard. Further, a Maritime Security Advisory Board (MSAB) and an Advisor (MSA) – again of the rank of a Vice Admiral in command – has also been sanctioned. Unless proper restraint is exercised, this may lead to clashes between the two commands.

The government is all set to launch more coastal police stations and intensive coastal vigil and combined patrolling at sea is on the cards. The Customs have procured state-of-the-art patrol boats from abroad and commenced intensive patrolling along vulnerable coastal areas. These boats can stay at sea for three consecutive days and the government is planning to add a few more to the existing fleet. As these measures have long term gestation periods, the various law enforcement departments may have to continue with the existing facilities for a while.

However, patrolling over the seas will have to be stepped up soon. Registration of all fishing boats has to be undertaken on a war footing. All fishing boats, MSVs and minor vessel traffic are to be marshaled through predetermined points.

As part of International Ships and Port Facility Security

(ISPS) Code, it has been made mandatory to fix certain identification equipments on board ships plying in international waters. These include the Automatic Identification System (AIS) up to 100 nautical miles with effect from July 1, 2004. Also, the Long Range Identification and Tracking (LRIT) System is set between 500-700 nautical miles with effect from January 1, 2009. The identification of the vessels and other relevant details could be used to track suspect ships.

Indian Space Research Organisation (ISRO) has developed a disaster beacon to track the location of fishing crafts in coastal waters. This is a substitute for the mandatory EPIRB (Emergency Position Indicating Radio Beacon) installed on almost all vessels out at sea. This beacon could also be utilised for identification at sea.

GVK Unnithan is a serving Master Mariner of the Mercantile Marine.

He is associated with International Maritime Security Training and retired as commander from the Indian Navy.

17
Foreign Agencies

On November 29, a crack team of America's Federal Bureau of Investigation landed in Mumbai airport from its Los Angeles and Washington office. As a rule, the FBI officials carry weapons wherever they go for assignments across the world. The FBI team had accepted the Indian government's invitation to help the Mumbai police with their investigations. But, the FBI team was in for a rude shock. The Indian customs siezed their weapons and asked them to clarify why they were carrying weapons into India. The FBI officials contacted their local office to talk to top officials in the Indian bureaucracy. It was only after the intervention of top officials in New Delhi that that they could walk out of the Mumbai airport with their weapons.

The FBI team immediately started meeting with Mumbai officials. An FBI official later told American Congress about the lessons learned from the Mumbai attacks to protect the U.S. As per the American laws, the FBI has to probe the death of any American citizen outside of the

U.S. and later submit a charge sheet, to try the case in the U.S. courts. This is the second case after the IC-814 hijacking case in which the FBI had registered a case in India as one of its citizens, Jeanne Moore, was in the Indian Airlines aircraft at that time. Interestingly, before the *fidayeen* attacks, the FBI never took previous terror attacks on Mumbai seriously. They were of the view that local Muslims were fighting with local Hindus over the Babri Masjid demolition and the Gujarat riots. Which is why, when an Indian journalist asked an FBI official why they did not categorise earlier attacks on Mumbai along with the Bali, Madrid or London bombings, the official said that the serial bombings in India were a local problem and that India should learn to deal with it.

After 26/11, this theory was proved wrong. Mumbai was now in the global terror network of Al Qaeda and it seemed to be the tip of the iceberg.

The FBI is now increasingly called upon to address criminal and *fidayeen* threats to U.S. interests in countries across the globe. Thanks to advances in technology, communications, and transportation, international boundaries have blurred a lot in the past decade. The FBI, which is one of the most respected security agencies, is asked to help local police forces by the American consulates, due to the domain knowledge they have acquired in the last few years. The FBI has helped the Pakistan police with Marriott bombings in Islamabad and the Kenyan police with the bombings of America's consulates.

The FBI says that to effectively combat international crime and terrorism, significant cooperation among law enforcement, domestic security, and intelligence agencies is required on a global scale. The FBI's effort to strengthen and expand foreign partnerships in the fight against global crime and terror is coordinated by its Office of International Operations (OIO) at the FBI Headquarters and carried out by the network of FBI Legal Attaché Offices, located in U.S. Embassies around the world. The FBI official in the host nations create an informal network of informers who give them information about local gangs.

In the event of a threat to, or actual attack against U.S. citizens or interests abroad – and after coordination with the Ambassador and host nation – the FBI usually deploys its investigative personnel and equipment and begins its extraterritorial investigation. The Counter-terrorism Division, for example, has the lead for the FBI's investigation of *fidayeen* attacks on U.S. citizens and interests overseas, as Mumbai attacks of November 26, 2008, which resulted in the deaths of six American citizens. The division head reports to the FBI director in Washington.

According to the FBI, the primary role of OIO and the Legal Attaches is to help the FBI's national security and law enforcement missions by promoting close working relations with its foreign law enforcement and security service counterparts in every region of the world. It is these relationships that directly result in foreign government cooperation and facilitation of FBI investigative activities abroad.

These relationships pay additional dividends in the form of prompt and continuous exchanges of information, which greatly contribute to its proactive efforts at terrorism prevention, the FBI says.

In the aftermath of significant incidents abroad affecting American citizens or interests, the FBI, through its local or regional Legal Attaché, extends an offer of investigative assistance to the senior leadership of the host-country law enforcement or domestic security partner.

According to a submission made by the FBI to the US Congress, such offers of assistance typically result in varying levels of foreign government law enforcement cooperation, consistent with all host-country legal requirements and with full regard to the sovereign interests of the host government. This basic formula describes the FBI's engagement in virtually all investigations of significant extraterritorial incidents, including the Mumbai terror attacks. For example, in the Mumbai attacks, the threads of investigations go as far as Pakistan, Afghanistan and Egypt where Indian investigating agencies has absolutely no reach or contacts.

In the Mumbai investigation, the contacts FBI's Legal Attaché in New Delhi had with Indian law enforcement and intelligence partners, as well as the quality of the investigative team led by the FBI's Counter-terrorism Division, had resulted in good cooperation. For example, within hours of the Mumbai attacks, the FBI obtained approval from the Government of India and the U.S. Embassy in New Delhi to deploy the Los Angeles Rapid

Deployment Team and several critical personnel from FBI's headquarters in Washington to Mumbai.

The FBI's objective was to assist the Indian government with its investigation, determine who was responsible for the deaths of Americans in the attacks, uncover any possible U.S. nexus to the attacks and any other related threats to U.S. citizens or interests abroad, and share intelligence and other lessons learned with rest of the U.S. intelligence and law enforcement communities.

The FBI Legal Attaché and Assistant Legal Attaché based in New Delhi also traveled to Mumbai to meet their Indian counterparts, to offer any assistance it needed, and support the incoming team. By December 17, 2008, several additional FBI personnel were deployed to Mumbai to assist in the local investigation.

In addition, FBIHQ and FBI LA established a 24 hour command posts to support the FBI team in Mumbai. These command posts also helped to process information obtained from the investigation and related interviews, as well as process tactical and strategic analysis to define the overall intelligence picture.

After the airport *faux pas*, the Indian government gave unprecedented access to evidence and intelligence related to the attacks from the Mumbai police and the Intelligence Bureau to the FBI. The FBI was provided access to most of the attack locations and technical evidence recovered from the scenes. The FBI officials also met the lone survivor of the attacks, Ajmal Kasab to understand the background and training imparted to him. The FBI was able to use advanced forensic and technical exploitation techniques to develop critical leads for both the Indian and U.S. investigations. The FBI also conducted more than 60 interviews of individuals in Mumbai, including witnesses with firsthand accounts of the attacks and security personnel who were involved in responding to the attacks.

According to the FBI, Ajmal Kasab claimed that the Pakistan-based fidayeen organization Lashkar-e-Toiba (LeT) provided him training and direction for the attack. The FBI assessed that LeT, which is well known to the U.S. Intelligence Community remains a threat to U.S. interests in South Asia. Though FBI has established that LeT has no presence in the United States, it found that it does maintain a facilitation, procurement, fundraising, and recruitment activities worldwide, including in the United States.

For example, in the last few years, the FBI said the US courts convicted several followers of the "Virginia Jihad" Network of providing material support to terrorism relating to their training at an LeT-sponsored training camp in Pakistan, with the intention of fighting against Coalition Forces in Afghanistan. In addition, the FBI is investigating a few individuals across the United States who are linked in some way to LeT–primarily through witting or unwitting fundraising for the group, as well as the recruitment of individuals from the United States to attend LeT camps abroad.

The FBI did not go home empty hand. It learnt an important lesson from the Mumbai attacks which in fact reinforces the notion that a small number of trained and determined attackers with relatively unsophisticated weapons can do a great deal of damage. It said other *fidayeen* groups, to include Al-Qaeda and its affiliates, will no doubt take note of the Mumbai attacks and attempt to emulate them.

It said the planning for the Mumbai attacks probably unfolded over a fairly long period with careful surveillance of the target sites and transportation routes.

The FBI would continue to work closely with its state, local, and tribal law enforcement partners, especially in its Joint Terrorism Task Forces to follow up on indications of suspicious activity that could potentially be related to terrorism. Similarly, it said that they would carefully monitor travel to participate in *fidayeen* activities or fighting overseas, such as that recently reported by ethnic Somalis traveling to fight in Somalia.

As the experience of the United Kingdom indicates, individuals who receive *fidayeen* training or experience overseas clearly represent a threat. In addition, the FBI said it needs to continue to heighten the public's awareness to the continued threat of *fidayeen* attacks and the need to report suspicious incidents. The FBI said whenever possible, all information was shared with the Indian government to aid in its investigation. The FBI disseminated more than 15 intelligence reports to the US Intelligence based on information collected in Mumbai from both interviews and physical evidence. The FBI said that another lesson learned from the Mumbai attacks is that *fidayeen* groups that appear to be primarily a threat to their surrounding localities can sometimes have broader aspirations. Although LeT has historically focused its attacks against Indian forces in the Kashmir region, the Mumbai attacks reinforce the reality that LeT has the capability to operate outside its home base.

The group did so in 2001 with an attack on the Indian Parliament building in New Delhi and is suspected of having been involved in the 2006 Mumbai train bombings. These actions highlight the need to examine other groups that appear to be active only locally and determine whether they have the operational capability and strategic intention to undertake a more regional or global agenda, the FBI's findings said.

The FBI is continuing its investigation in Mumbai and has asked to interview other individuals in Indian custody who may be able to provide critical information on attack planning and group leadership.

The FBI's counter-terrorism agents and analysts are working to analyse all available information on the Mumbai attacks in order to determine who was responsible, assess lessons learned, determine if the United States may be vulnerable to a similar attack, and determine the threat posed by the group – or individuals tied to the group – to the United States.

It was thanks to the FBI's role in investigating the Mumbai

terror attacks that India and the U.S. managed to recover credible evidence against the LeT. *The Times of India* quoted outgoing U.S. Ambassador David Mulford saying that that the evidence dossier, shared with the international community, has details of the trail of evidence that traces the origin of the attack back to Pakistan and the LeT. The dossier includes transcripts of calls between the ten *fidayeens* and their handlers in Pakistan, a list of 'Made in Pakistan' items, photographs of the weapons used in the attacks, and the GPS equipment carried by the *fidayeens*.

The FBI team also travelled to Pakistan to follow these and other leads that have emerged in the case. "They are finishing some things here. We do wish to interview certain people... That has to be worked out with the Pakistani government," Mr Mulford said. The FBI team is looking for LeT operations commander Zaki-ur-Rehman Lakhvi, the suspected mastermind behind the attacks, and LeT commander Zarar Shah.

In spite of evidence, however, there was frustration in Washington on Pakistan's responses after the Mumbai attacks. "In Washington there is a measure of frustration and concern about responses, but there is also measure of satisfaction with some of the things we have heard," Mr Mulford said. He emphasised that India and Pakistan need to work together against terrorism. "What was disturbing was that the attack was carried out from the territory of Pakistan. What's most important to us is that India and Pakistan should seek to work together because it is a *fidayeen* probe. Terrorism doesn't know any boundaries. But cooperation is becoming increasingly difficult as Islamabad has refused to accept any of the evidence given by India," Mr Mulford told the paper.

In spite of the painstaking work done by the FBI and the evidence presented to the Pakistan government, its Prime Minister downplayed the significance of evidence on the Mumbai attacks, saying it only contained information and "not evidence". Pakistan has acknowledged that the only surviving Mumbai gunman was Pakistani, but it insists that none of its state agencies played a role in the attacks. Under international pressure, Pakistan has detained some suspects allegedly linked to the attacks, while repeatedly calling on India to provide evidence to allow legal prosecutions.

The dossier, handed over on January 5, includes transcripts of phone calls allegedly made during the siege by the attackers and their handlers in Pakistan. Previously, India had given Pakistan a letter from the lone surviving gunman, Mohammed Ajmal Kasab that reportedly said he and the nine other gunmen were Pakistani. On January 9, the U.S. Vice President elect Joe Biden even held talks in Pakistan as part of a regional tour expected to focus on terrorism and tensions between Pakistan and India following the Mumbai attacks. But it did not serve any purpose. Pakistan continues to remain in a state of denial.

18
Why Mumbai?

A few weeks after 26/11, the Prime Minister of India, Dr Manmohan Singh, said that the attacks were part of a larger conspiracy to destabilise the Indian economy. Mumbai, home to India's largest corporates, banks and financial institutions, signifies the growing economic power of the country. Though the PM was not saying anything new, it just sums up the motive of the attacks.

The city's skyline is changing fast with its property prices now hovering in line with international cities. It is common knowledge in the country that anyone who wants to make money should start in Mumbai. The city is brimming with rags to riches stories and migrants from across the country keep streaming into the city.

In spite of new, emerging cities like Bengaluru, Hyderabad and Pune, the ever increasing charm of Mumbai keeps attracting people. Ever since India embarked on economic reforms, the inflow of people and wealth just shot ahead by leaps and bounds.

The PM said that India would not accept a situation where terrorism is used as an instrument to cripple its economy or the values it stands for. The PM also indicated a larger design behind the Mumbai attacks, for which India has blamed Pakistan-based elements. "The non-state actors were practising terrorism aided and abetted by state establishments. The removal of poverty and emancipation of our people should be given the place of pride in India's foreign policy," the PM said.

Officers in the Indian intelligence agencies say that as the top Indian corporates based in Mumbai and investors from across the world are now making a beeline to set up shop in the city, the larger plan of the terrorists was to sabotage the city's growing power. A report by noted economist, Percy Mistry has already been submitted to the Government of India on how to make the city the next financial capital of the world situated between Singapore in the east and Dubai in the west. The PM said that the attacks showed the risk all countries face from economic sabotage "irrespective of whether these acts are authored by states or merely carried out by so-called non-state actors (read ISI)."

The External Affairs Minister, Mr Pranab Mukherjee also echoed the PM's view as he said that the aim of the *fidayeens* was to harm India's economic growth and its growing economic influence across the world. As the world drowned in deep recession in 2008, the only country that recorded a healthy 7% growth was India. Clearly, the target was the Indian economy and the attacks on the luxury hotels was to scare away foreign investors.

The government also realised that apart from protecting its borders from foreign intruders, it is imperative to provide good security cover to trade and industry. Soon after the attacks, the government raised the issue of terror threats against vital energy installations at the Petrotech 2009 conference. The External Affairs Minister said that the hydrocarbon sector had to be better prepared against such attacks and that oil and gas installations and the connected transport infrastructure should be safeguarded. The minister pointed out that protecting such energy installations, which include pipelines, is not just the task of one country but would requirea coordinated, international effort.

In the background, one of the biggest casualties was the ambitious pipeline project to import gas from Iran via the land route in Pakistan. The government sources say that till the security of an oil and gas pipeline over Pakistan is completely assured by the local governments, the project would never take off. Soon after the attacks, one of the steps that the government is interested in taking forward is of deploying government forces to protect key vital installations in the light of the growing threat of *fidayeens*.

The security of Bombay High oil fields was upgraded soon after the attacks and its safety was handed over to the Indian Navy and the Coast Guard. Similarly, the oil refineries belonging to a private sector company in Gujarat installed anti-aircraft guns.

P Chidambaram, the Finance Minister turned Home Minister, said a day after the attacks that the Indian economy will "overcome" the impact of the terror attacks. Chidambaram predicted India's growth would rebound to 9 percent from as low as 7 percent this year. Even at 7 percent, Chidambaram says India's growth is three times the rate of global expansion and is second only to China among major economies.

But the terror attacks really hurt the travel and tourism industry in India. Tourist arrivals during January to April 2009 were expected to fall almost 25-30%. A survey by PHD Chamber in North India showed that there has been a 50% fall in outbound tourism. Business tourism has also taken a beating as outbound and corporate incentive tours have fallen. In October this year, there was a mere 1.8% rise in the number of foreign tourists coming to India over the corresponding figure for October 2007.

A travel alert by the U.S. government scared away tourists. The Department of State warned U.S. citizens about heightened security concerns in India, and advised U.S. citizens travelling to, or already in India, to maintain a high level of vigilance and to take appropriate steps to increase their security awareness. It said that while *fidayeen* attacks were not new to India, the 26/11 Mumbai *fidayeen* attacks, in part, targeted American citizens and other Westerners for the first time and demonstrated that even in five-star luxury hotels, security was not well-equipped to deter such attacks. The alert asked U.S. citizens to take into account this new reality and exercise caution when visiting India.

Prudent security measures include maintaining a high level of vigilance, avoiding crowds and demonstrations and keeping a low profile by not calling attention to one's nationality, advised the government.

The Department of State also advised its citizens planning to travel to Mumbai in the aftermath of the *fidayeen* attacks to recognise that it may be some time before all public infrastructure and services returned to normal. The alert said that emotions are running high and there are possibilities of demonstrations which could turn violent.

No wonder then the attackers clearly wanted to change the image of Mumbai from a safe, healthy and welcoming business destination to that, say of, Beirut or Kabul.

Compare Mumbai to any other business destination in the region. Terrorists cannot target China as the government is quite tough on Muslim terrorism. Many leaders of terror outfits from China's Xinjiang region were just picked up and shot just before the Olympics began. Similarly, the governments of Singapore and Dubai would just eliminate threats before they even land in the city.

Mumbai, on the other hand, is a soft target. The city has porous borders. Anyone can walk into the city from the country. The infiltration of Bangladeshi nationals into the city is continuous and the politicians are too busy fighting with each other to bother about checking the antecedents of the new arrivals. The city provides lots of employment opportunities and migrants can settle almost immediately in cheap slums sprouting across the city.

The top officials of the city police are fighting with each other even as corruption is eating into the entire system. It is a common sight in Mumbai to witness a policeman on beat duty collecting money from hawkers and illegal stall owners. In spite of bomb blasts in the local trains only two years ago, the security at public places is still lax. The intelligence agencies in the country kept repeating similar and non-actionable reports that are immediately relegated to the waste paper basket. Thus, the city has been in fact inviting such an attack since none of the agencies is interested in protecting the common man.

Soon after the attacks, the top officials in the finance ministry said the impact of the attacks would be temporary and short term. However, the image of the city as a financial centre has taken a severe beating. Many investors postponed their visits to Mumbai. Although not a single project moved out of the city, the Mumbai attacks scared away many potential investors.

19
Ill-Prepared Mumbai Police

The Mumbai police force was not prepared to face anything like the multiple and simultaneous attacks the *fidayeens* had planned. The terrorists were able to create a lot of mayhem since the police did not manage to stop them soon enough.

The attackers carried AK-56 assault rifles, a Chinese copy of the Russian 47s. The deadly weapon has the capacity to fire around 600 rounds per minute. The local police were armed with .38 caliber pistols and 9 mm government factory made Brownings. Few had SLRs and AK-47 assault rifles, but not many were used against the LeT operatives.

There was also a major difference in the mental makeup of the *fidayeens* and the police. While the *fidayeens* were willing to sacrifice their lives for a cause, for many policemen doing anything to stop them was suicidal. They knew that they could not take on the heavily armed attackers and it was more important to save their own lives.

The plans made by the police, had left much to be desired. There was no leader that night to guide the policemen to challenge the *fidayeens* and pin them down at the earliest. Tactically, they were taking things as it came.

Although the policemen were immediately mobilised on the streets, they were no match to the superior weapons and the confusing tactics the gunmen used. Many policemen had not heard the crack of an automatic weapon in years. Yet, the Mumbai police braved bullets to prevent any further loss of life in the city. It took almost 10 hours before the commandos were ready for action and the city police therefore had to engage the *fidayeens*, who had learnt their tactics from those fighting Indian security forces in Kashmir for more than a decade.

The attackers worked together as a team, they had a lot of stamina and continued their attack for several hours. Worse still, the local policemen were faced with an enemy who knew their targets better than the naval marine commandos and NSG commandos.

Moreover, they functioned as 'buddy pairs' which is generally taught at military commando training schools across the country. The *fidayeens* were also taught to mystify and misdirect police operations, as exhibited during the attack on luxury hotels in South Mumbai. They kept hopping from one floor to the other giving the impression that there were many of them. The police, on the other hand, did not have a plan and were trying to launch a frontal attack. The senior officers were distracted and so were the juniors.

Initially, the policemen underestimated the seriousness of the attacks on Leopold and the lane behind the Taj Mahal Hotel. "We thought it was an exchange of fire between two gangs of drug traffickers at Colaba," said Joint Commissioner of Police Rakesh Maria.

Despite the fact there were dozens of blasts across the city in the past few years and many point to the involvement of Pakistani Inter Service Intelligence operatives in connivance with other groups, it is surprising that the Mumbai police were not prepared to challenge *fidayeens*.

Neither the police, nor the intelligence officials thought that a group of highly motivated *fidayeens* would sail around 500 nautical miles and attack targets in the city. The LeT operatives had done the impossible, which made it even more unexpected. Moreover, they kept changing their tactics after talking to their handlers over mobile phones and other communication devices.

The *fidayeens* were well-trained and knew a lot about the intelligence and capabilities of the Mumbai police. The LeT functionaries had drawn a perfect strategic plan, which was carried out in clockwork precision. The planning that culminated in the Mumbai terror attacks succeeded because it was a classic manoeuvre employing all the elements of surprise.

One glaring error has been that there was no leader for the Mumbai police. The demoralised force needed a strong leader to see through the terror attacks.

The death of Joint Commissioner of Police Hemant Karkare, Additional Commissioner Ashok Kamte and Inspector Vijay Salaskar, and the death of Assistant Police Sub-Inspector Tukaram Omble are classic examples of unplanned frontal attacks. The brave officers were barely able to establish contact with the *fidayeens* before engaging them in gun battles. Many had exposed themselves to the attacker's bullets. In fact, all were victims of ambush – common tactics imparted to *fidayeens* in Pakistan, Afghanistan and Iraq.

The Mumbai police was pushing outward with an untrained force and lacked unity in command. There were no tactics in place to engage the attackers in one-to-one confrontation. Encirclement tactics were not used. It was a kind of street war with the *fidayeen* moving from building to building while fighting. It was necessary for the police to throw a ring around the war zone so that they could not escape.

It was at around midnight of November 26 that the top brass of Mumbai police realised that the situation had gone out of control and it was time to get the specialised forces to swing into action. Maharashtra Chief Secretary Johnny Joseph was requested to seek the help of Marine Commandos (MARCOS), the Army and the National Security Guard (NSG).

Joseph immediately alerted the western naval command and asked them to send the Marcos. Subsequently, Joseph also made a call to the NSG director J K Dutta in Delhi briefing him about the situation and asked him to rush the NSG commandoes to Mumbai.

In spite of the call from Joseph at midnight, it was well past 2 am when two columns (each consisting of seven fighters) of Marcos finally reached the two luxury hotels. On reaching the two hotels, the Marcos refused to enter the hotels in absence of any authorisation from the state. (The Navy has however denied this).

Another goof up by the Marcos was that within hours of the operation they announced that two *fidayeens* inside the Taj had been killed in the operation. This information later turned out to be incorrect.

The NSG team took a long time to reach Mumbai because they had to arrange for an aircraft to fly them to Mumbai. The aircraft was to come from Chandigarh to Delhi pick the NSG team and air dash them to Mumbai.

The NSG finally landed in Mumbai at around 4.20 am on November 27. By the time they took over the operation it was 9 am. Once the NSG came in, the Marcos backed out as they refused to function under an NSG Brigadier.

The one-upmanship of the senior defence officials reached a new low, when they went live on national news networks even while the gunfight was on. Senior army officials briefed the media persons and told them that there were atleast a dozen *fidayeens* inside the Taj Mahal Hotel.

Like the police, even the NSG's 30-odd member Quick Response Team were almost out of plans or tactics to close in on the *fidayeen*. They did not have a strong-hearted officer who could lead them through the ensuing gun battles.

Meanwhile, the helpless people of Mumbai watched their city bleed.

20
Mumbai Police: A Demoralised Force Cut A Sorry Figure

While the ten *fidayeens* were in training camps for 18 months, the policemen in Mumbai had not fired a gun even once after graduating from the academy. Even more shocking: only one in every 10 policemen went for firing practice. Nor were they referred to attend refresher courses or advanced weapon training, which could boost their morale during actual confrontations with criminals on the streets of Mumbai. Regular training helps build confidence, which was evidently missing during 26/11 and in the days that followed.

The manner in which the force was mobilised in South Mumbai indicated that there was no overall strategic plan. Also, the way in which the force was deployed showed lack of tactical and support plan. Senior officers did not have a plan of attack or any alternate tactics.

Commissioner of Police Hasan Gafoor was very sympathetic about his officers and men, many of whom laid down their lives during the attacks. "They volunteered to face the enemy with only lathis or sticks. In other countries no force would move out without backup or adequate support," remarked the Indian Police Service officer.

The terror attacks in Mumbai brought to the fore a total lack of training and readiness to react to any situation or attack at the shortest notice. The seniors could not expect too much from their poorly paid force or whip them into shape for military-like jobs. Most of them are bogged down with routine jobs at police stations and many of them are deployed as attendants to the Indian Police Service officers. Even senior inspectors have at least two policemen to attend to their mundane needs.

The senior officers themselves have virtually no experience in counter-terrorism methods. Not many of them have undergone weapons training in the past few years.

The Mumbai attack is considered one of the most memorable security lapses of the force. This is mainly because of the lack of informers.

The last time a LeT module was busted when a Crime Intelligence Unit (CIU) team killed three members of a hit team at Goregoan on May 27, 2003. The officers were working on remarkable HUMINT or human intelligence, which was the hallmark of the crime branch in the late 1990s.

HUMINT is the use of human assets for gathering

information. The person could be an informer, contact or an agent who is monitored for the collection of information in the interest of national security. It could be collecting information on underworld gangs too.

By 2003, dozens of crime branch officers were bogged down with court cases and many were even shunted out of the elite department. HUMINT suffered as the information network was disturbed. Informants did not find it safe to work with new groups of officers, since it takes years of building trust before an informant can become an asset for the officer or the police.

Over the past few years, police officers have been depending on electronic interceptions. This has reduced dependence on local informants or *khabris* as they are known in underworld circles.

Gathering information on *fidayeens* is not easy. Officers may have to draw huge amounts from the Secret Service Funds to motivate *khabris* to go on the terror trail. Also the investigating team should have sufficient inputs, which could be shared with the informant.

"The informant should be indoctrinated and trained before he should set out on the task related to national security. He should know what to look for and where. In fact, the task can become extremely difficult when one is faced with a faceless enemy and very little chance for infiltration. More so, if suspects on the watch lists are from hostile areas across the border," informed a field officer from a central intelligence agency. Electronic surveillance, on the other hand, is very sophisticated. It can make the task of gathering information easy, but it has its limitations.

END OF UNDERWORLD, RISE OF TERRORISM

The end of 2001 saw a decline in criminal gangs in the city. In retrospect, this led to a breakdown in intelligence gathering networks the police had painstakingly set up, and indicated a subsequent drop in police morale. Almost all organised gangs had been decimated by the police. More than 600 gangsters had been shot dead across the city in encounters between 1996 and 2002.

Several encounter squads had gone on a rampage, killing dozens of gangsters on the streets of Mumbai every month. It brought in a windfall for the informants, who provided inside information on the gangsters.

Over the years, the entire campaign to halt the rise of the underworld has been carried out by a handful of officers. The first encounter in the city dates back to 1981, when a special squad comprising Isaque Bagwan, Sunil Temkar, Shamsher Khan Pathan, and Emanual Amolik gunned down urban dacoit Manya Surve. These officers were in the forefront while dealing with the gang war between the Dawood Ibrahim and the Pathan gang led by Amirzada and Alamzeb in the early 1980s.

The early batch of crime branch officers saw the rise the D Company till 1987. It was about the same time militancy was on the rise and makeshift squads set up by then

Commissioner of Police Julio Riberio were made active. Officers like Ambadas Pote, Sunil Deshmukh, Praful Joshi, Kiran Sonane, Prakash George and A Kavi were active in cornering gangsters in and around Mumbai, although on a lesser scale and not on a regular basis. Some of the officers even joined the Anti-*Fidayeen* Squad under the command of Additional Commissioner of Police A A Khan. The operation at Lokhandwala Complex where gangsters Dilip Buva and Maya Dolas were gunned down was one of their biggest successes.

Of the 600-odd gangsters killed in Mumbai over the past two decades, it is almost certain that each time the gangster was eliminated by a squad, officers of the 1983 batch of sub-inspectors were involved. Officers like Praful Bhosle, Vijay Salaskar, Ravindranath Aangre, Pradeep Sharma, and Arun Borude became the nemesis of members of the underworld. There were others like Arun Kenjale, Rajan Bhogle, Sharad Rao who were in equally important capacities in dealing with the underworld menace. Most officers from this 1983 batch of officers saw action soon after underworld activities were hotting up since Rajan Nikalje had split from his mentor Dawood Ibrahim in 1993.

Many encounter specialists were back to the crime branch after stints in various police stations by 1992-93. The daring operations during the riots and serial blasts added to their list of achievements. However, the actual crackdown through encounters started when ex-army officer Ramdeo Tyagi took charge as Police Commissioner in 1996 and peaked under Joint Commissioner D

Sivanandhan and Deputy Commissioner Pradip Sawant. Stoic and silent R H Mendonca and his former colleague from the army Ranjit Singh Sharma continued to mount pressure on the underworld.

Then Deputy Commissioner of Police Dr Satya Pal Singh and Param Bir Singh had also formed separate squads where most of today's encounter specialists were inducted and groomed. Their forays decimated the Arun Gawli, Chhota Rajan and Dawood Ibrahim gangs. Even commissioner of police M N Singh used police shooters to turn on the heat on the underworld.

Even as the vintage specialists of '83 batch' were busy adding up the head count, juniors like Hemant Desai, Avinash Sawant, Mahesh Desai, Prakash Bhandari, Ashok Khot, Bhushan Belnekar, Ninad Sawant, Sanjeev Gawde, and Daya Nayak had received training to follow in their footsteps. By 2002, the gangs were almost wiped out from the city. Encounter levels slipped down to low levels, almost 10 percent. There were only five encounters reported in 2004.

The encounter specialists were always on target and the manner in which the gangs were eliminated is interesting. After the 1993 serial blasts, members of the Dawood Ibrahim gang were on top on the hitlist of the encounter specialists. Dawood lost 15 frontline shooters in encounters that year. The reasons were not unclear.

Dawood's former lieutenant, Rajendra Nikalje aka Chhota Rajan, was now among the upper echelons of Mumbai's underworld. Rajan also professed patriotism among his core group and it found favour with Indian intelligence. It was not long before Rajan's men were used to eliminate some accused named in the 1993 blasts. He has assumed the mantle of a 'Hindu don' and was considered close to many crime branch officers in Mumbai.

Rival gangsters Arun Gawli lost 33 shooters soon after he floated the Akhil Bhartiya Sena in 1996. Dawood Ibrahim on the other hand lost 86 frontline shooters between 1995-99. The Chhota Rajan gang lost 92 gangsters between 2000 and 2005. Dawood's losses were restricted to only 42 during the same period.

A clear pattern had emerged. Particular gangs were eliminated with every change in the government. Rules were changed several times and posts were upgraded to suit the appointment of Mumbai's Commissioner of Police and the Director General of Police in the last few years.

With the elimination of the gangs, the encounter specialists soon lost their importance. The intelligence gathering network they had developed over the years was of very little use to them now. The scenario was swiftly changing and *fidayeens* trained in camps in Pakistan became active in Mumbai. There were dozens of bomb blasts across the country.

The encounter specialists were caught unawares and many were kept off investigations. Their problems were further compounded when departmental inquiries were slammed against them. What the top brass failed to realise was that the men they had groomed to finish the underworld were a creation of the system. The officers who were once encouraged to kill were now indicted, some on corruption charges. Politics within the department added more fuel to the fire.

The morale of the policemen touched its lowest when at least three senior Indian Police Officers were booked under MCOCA. They were faced with corruption charges in the fake stamps case that rocked the state in 2003. But, the Mumbai police received a shock when an improvised explosive device ripped through a BEST bus in Ghatkopar on December 2, 2002. This was quickly followed by a series of blasts across the city in the next four months.

It was during the interrogation of a few suspects that the crime branch officers learnt that a large number of wanted men had secretly slipped into *fidayeen* camps in Pakistan for training. Dozens of names emerged during investigations. What was even more shocking was that many did not have a criminal record. Even worse, almost all of them had university backgrounds. Some were engineers and doctors.

Weapons introduced during the *fidayeen* training were the latest range of assault rifles like AK-56, AK-74, G2, and G3 used by the Indian and Pakistani army. The trainees were taught to use Rocket Propelled Guns (RPG) such as RPG 2 and RPG 7, and all kinds of 7.62 mm calibre pistols mostly manufactured in China.

The suspects yielded information about how they had travelled to Pakistan via Bangladesh and Nepal. The documents were forged and almost all were given fake identities. In some cases, recruits were sent to camps through Dubai. Investigators also learnt that some terror suspects were induced to enlist as *jihadis* when they were employed in Gulf countries. The immigrant labourers were whisked away to training camps in Pakistan before they could return to India.

What the Mumbai police failed to grasp was the fact all recruits were introduced to the Al Qaeda manual. They were taught how to level false allegations against law enforcement agencies so as to put them under the pressure of courts. They received training on how to accept responsibility of a blast or attack, to subterfuge investigations and even create confusion among the rank and file of the police force.

The state government had failed to take a serious view of the Al Qaeda manual. Politicians did not realise that the Al Qaeda could be behind the financing of several militant groups operating in Pakistan.

The police and the politicians failed to see the new challenges posed by the terror groups. Despite the decline of gang wars in the city, the police could not use the time available to train themselves in counter-terrorism techniques.

Most of the officers in Mumbai were still focusing on a few splinter gangs and robbers. Serial blasts on suburban trains in 2006 failed to change their mindset. Intelligence Bureau's advice and tip-offs were seldom heeded.

The coordination between ATS and the city's crime branch has left much to be desired. In fact, there are no clear lines of demarcation that divides the two elite police teams in the city.

Almost two months after the attacks, Mumbai police is yet to cope with the shift in tactics: from suicide bombings and blasts, to commando style sustained attacks by a small group of highly trained operatives.

Mumbai police administration on the other hand has set up bunkers across the city. They have intensified *nakabandis* – random checking of vehicles on the road. The local police have yet to shift their focus from crime-fighting to systematic intelligence gathering. They have yet to find a way out to prevent Mumbai-based gangsters and *fidayeens* from talking to their handlers in neighbouring countries over cell phones and other communication devices. A counter-terrorism team is yet to be formed with infrastructure protection capabilities and other important issues like intelligence collection. The team should also specialise in port and maritime security.

21
Previous Attacks And The Legal Tangle

Mumbai has the distinction of being the most attacked and bombed city in the world. From 1990, there have been close to 100 bomb blasts that have ripped the city apart, killing more than 700 people and injuring more than 2000 innocents.

Experts say that the reason Mumbai has been targeted over and over again is because anything done in Mumbai makes international news. If *fidayeens* have to get a point across, then the easiest way is to attack Mumbai.

The bomb blasts that first made international news were the March 1993 serial bomb blasts. Within minutes, twelve bomb blasts tore Mumbai apart by those seeking revenge for the Babri Masjid demolitions on December 6, 1992 and the 1992-93 riots. The serial bomb blasts case was the longest running case in the history of India. More than 123 accused, including Bollywood actor Sanjay Dutt, were tried by a special court which heard the case for a mammoth 15 long years.

Finally, in 2007, the court convicted almost 100 accused in the case. However, the feeling still remains that those who were convicted were second rung members in the conspiracy. The main perpetrators of the bomb blasts, including fugitive underworld don Dawood Ibrahim, Tiger Memon, and others were never brought to book.

After that the city was bombed several times by local and international radicals trying to prove a point. Then came the big one – July 11, 2006 – the bombs on Mumbai's lifeline – the local trains. Here again, the radicals sent out a message that they wanted revenge for the Godhra riots and the killings of innocents by Indian security forces in Jammu and Kashmir.

The theory put forth by the police was that groups of local Student's Islamic Movement of India (SIMI) activists partnered by members of the LeT set the bombs in seven local trains. However, that theory is not likely to hold much credence in the court. Here too, the public opinion remains that this case will linger on for several years, with the main perpetrators never standing trial.

This has been the story of all terror attacks in the country. "Since almost all terror attacks have their roots in the neighbouring country, it becomes difficult for the police to investigate and interrogate the perpetrators beyond a point," says a senior central intelligence officer.

All the links and leads take the police beyond the country's border, and there is little that the police can do because they cannot go into another country and question or arrest suspects, especially when India does not have any extradition treaty with the neighbouring country.

As has been often lamented by the police, the archaic laws of India make it almost impossible for the enforcement agencies to get a conviction if the actual conspirators and bomb planters are not found. A look at all the cases pending in various courts of the country indicates that most cases are pending because the police have not yet been able to catch the actual planners.

And, the terror outfits have exploited this legal loophole to the hilt. The actual planners and conspirators are never sent on the field. While those who are sent on the field are never the planners, they are part of a module which is involved in the terror attacks only on a need-to-know basis. Therefore, even if any of them is caught by the police he will reveal only his involvement in that particular terror plot – this, in the Indian legal system, is not enough to convict a person.

The general feeling is that over a period of time everyone forgets the tragedy and gets on with life. Also, with bomb blasts and terror attacks in the country in such alarming regularity, the administration and law enforcement agencies do not have time for following up on pending cases.

Even though it took 15 years to get convictions in the 1993 serial bomb blast case, the case itself is far from over.

There are still some more accused who are being tried in the special court. And, unless the likes of Dawood Ibrahim and Tiger Memon are arrested, the case will never really be over. However, experts feel that Dawood Ibrahim may never be caught alive by the Indian police.

Some lesser known cases like the 1998 crude bombings in the western suburbs of Mumbai did reach its conclusion and the Sessions Court of Mumbai had convicted a few locals, but even that case is pending in the higher courts because the convicts have appealed.

Even if the police are able to catch the culprits, the legal system is so slow that by the time justice is delivered it is too late. A classic case in point is the conviction of 1993 serial bomb blast case, by the time the special court delivered justice, the convicts themselves had become old. Looking at the aging convicts there was a feeling of sympathy for them.

Most of the convicts who were sentenced to life imprisonment had already served more than their term (in India, life term generally extends till 14 years). Some of them who were sentenced to seven years or ten years and had already been in prison for more than the term walked free after the sentence was passed, making one feel that justice had not been done.

A glance through the status of other bomb blast cases tells a sad story – almost all major bomb blast cases are pending in courts. Some have been stayed by superior courts on technical grounds. While, the suspects (who may or may not be guilty) rust in jails as undertrails, the police, victims and witnesses go through the ordeal of attending courts and giving lengthy statements.

The government has time and again come up with several stringent laws with the intention of preventing further terror attacks and ensuring quick justice, but all the efforts have been half-hearted.

Laws like the Prevention Of Terrorist Activities (POTA) Act, Terrorist And Disruptive Activities (TADA) Act, Unlawful Activities Prevention Act (UAPA) and the Maharashtra Control of Organised Crime Act (MCOCA) have been enacted by the legislature after major terror attacks, but these acts either have many loopholes that have been exploited by suspects or have been misused by the law enforcement agencies. Some like the POTA and TADA became victims of communal politics.

The Al Qaeda manual which was reportedly seized by the Mumbai police from a bomb blast accused clearly outlines the guidelines which suspects should follow in the event of their arrest by the Indian police.

The manual says that in the event of an arrest of a *jehadi* by the Indian police, the *jehadi* will be produced in the court before a magistrate. When produced before the judge the *jehadi* should tell the court that he has been tortured by the police in custody. According to the Indian law, if an accused in custody complaints to the court of police torture, the court is duty bound to order an enquiry against the police. This will delay the case against the *jehadi*.

These and many such legal loopholes are exploited by *fidayeens* time and again.

However, as far as Mohammad Ajmal Amir alias Kasab, the lone arrested *fidayeen* is concerned, the police and legal experts feel that the case should not take long to reach a conclusion.

"It's an open-and-shut case," says Rakesh Maria, Joint Commissioner of Police and Chief of the Mumbai crime branch. Ajmal was captured live on video when he was firing randomly at innocent people on the CST railway station. He was also photographed by several people while he and his associate were walking in CST station. There are several eyewitnesses who saw Ajmal shooting with his AK-47 assault rifle.

The police are confident that they will be able to get a conviction based purely on the sections of the Indian Penal Code (IPC) and other stringent laws like the UAPA or MCOCA may not be required at all. Also, with the government setting up a fast track court for a speedy trial in the case, it is expected that the case may be over within a few weeks, unlike other bomb blast cases which may continue to gather dust for several years to come.

22
Lessons Learnt

One of the main lessons learnt from 26/11 is that none of the corporate headquarters, financial centres, or prime properties in the city are safe from suicide attacks. Even only two months after the attacks, not many corporates or banks have taken steps to increase security. Mumbai is still a vulnerable target as ever before.

A visit to the headquarters of the many corporates in this city or banks or even the Reserve Bank of India (the banking sector regulators) shows that the only changes made in security cover is cosmetic. The glass doors are now manned by a few more unarmed guards but very few companies are taking security seriously. Police patrolling has ceased again and the cops on the beat are back to collecting bribes from hawkers and stall owners. The security that was hastily set up after November 26 is back to square one, or rather, square zero.

A day after the attacks, the Chairman of the Tata group, Ratan Tata said that the city does not have crisis infrastructure. Two months after the attacks, the city is still not witnessing any signs of a crisis infrastructure. In an interview to CNN, Mr Tata said that the attacks revealed deficiencies in law enforcement, especially in areas of crisis response and management.

"We were getting the cooperation that they could give us, but the infrastructure was woefully poor," he said. Mr Tata said it took three hours for the firefighters to get water to the Taj after a blaze broke out in the oldest part of the building.

Mr Tata said that not even the army or the commandos who ultimately took over the offensive were prepared for the level of organisation and execution that the attackers seemed to have put into their plan.

He said that the attacks underscored the need for law enforcement to develop infrastructure for crisis management, even if it meant seeking outside expertise for training, equipment and strategic operations.

"We've been very complacent, because we've really not had this kind of terrorism inflicted upon us," he said. "We should not stand on ceremony to hold back. We should go to the best place possible to get expertise." Mr Tata was hopeful that the attacks would unite Indians for a common goal of preventing a similar tragedy. "Rather than have us succumb to this kind of terror, what it has done is given us a resolve that nobody can do this to us," he said.

Both the Taj, and the Trident-Oberoi did reopen within three weeks of having been attacked and raised the bar for entry into the hotel, but the city is still not prepared for an attack. Or even if an attack were to take place, how to react to it. Take for example, the railway stations, bus stops, and malls that are still extremely venerable to attacks. Assuming that another attack of similar scale takes place, the city is still unprepared.

Although the city has a vast unguarded sea front, it is also home to the Bhabha Atomic Research Centre (BARC), which has good security. However, media reports later showed that anyone could walk into the BARC through many holes in the walls.

The most important question to be raised now is – are we prepared for another attack? The answer to that is, no. The city has not learnt its lessons from 26/11. The city's common man, and not the politicians and money bags, are still vulnerable to attacks. Post 9/11, the U.S. took many steps to stop people from entering the country. But post 26/11, the city has still not come up with any plan to identify the antecedents of new arrivals.

It is the city's misfortune that none of the politicians have raised their voice against terror. No one has declared a war on terror. Instead the city has politicians who are busy dividing the citizens on the basis of their religion and caste. The army, NSG, and the Marine commandos went back to their barracks and the city is once again exposed to threats from attackers across the border.

Instead of blaming Pakistan for exporting terror, the Indian government should strive to raise barriers of entry to outsiders.

Sadly, the city of dreams is in perennial danger.